HERE AND
NOWHERE
ELSE

OTHER VOLUMES IN THE CONCORD LIBRARY

Series Editor: John Elder

Here and
Nowhere
Else

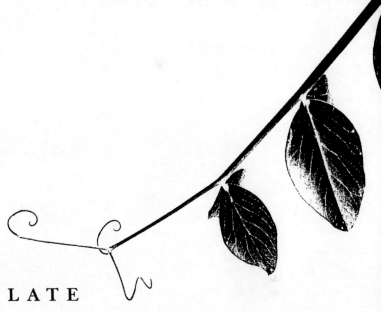

LATE

SEASONS OF A FARM

AND ITS FAMILY

Jane Brox

BEACON PRESS

BOSTON

Beacon Press
25 Beacon Street
Boston, Massachusetts 02108-2892
www.beacon.org

Beacon Press books
are published under the auspices of
the Unitarian Universalist Association of Congregations.

First digital-print edition 2002

Library of Congress Cataloging-in-Publication Data
Brox, Jane, 1956–
Here and nowhere else: late seasons of a farm and its family / Jane Brox
p.   cm.
ISBN 0-8070-6200-6 (cloth)
ISBN 0-8070-6201-4 (pbk.)
1. Brox, Jane, 1956–   —Homes and haunts—Merrimack Valley (N.H. and Mass.)
2. Women authors, American—20th century—Biography 3. Family farms—
Merrimack Valley (N.H. and Mass.) 4. Farm life— Merrimack Valley (N.H. and Mass.)
I. Title.
PS3552.R79125Z466   1995
818´.5403—dc20   94-36416

FOR MY FAMILY

Their care keeps us awake.
Their starry fear
shines in the tree of our speech.

—Johannes Bobrowski

CONTENTS

ACKNOWLEDGMENTS

Acknowledgment is due to the following publications where some of these pieces first appeared: *Fiction, The Georgia Review, The Gettysburg Review, Merrimack: A Poetry Anthology, New England Review, The Ohio Review, Salamander,* and *Taos Review.*

I'd like to thank the National Endowment for the Arts and the Massachusetts Cultural Council for literature grants, which gave me time to complete this book. Thanks also to The MacDowell Colony, Yaddo, The Millay Colony, VCCA, The Ucross Foundation, and The Banff Centre for providing quiet places to work.

Over the years many friends and teachers have given thoughtful attention to parts of this book, and to them I owe my deepest gratitude. Thanks in particular to Linda Hess, Kathy Aponick, E. F. Weisslitz, Paul Marion, and Maggie Brox for their encouragement, and to Martha Rhodes and Alan Brown for their attention to an earlier version of this manuscript. A debt of gratitude to Michael Ryan for first suggesting a form for these pieces, and to Thomas Lux and Heather McHugh for their guidance. Finally, I'd like to thank Deanne Urmy at Beacon for her clear-eyed intelligence and her unstinting support.

Prologue

WE LIVE thirty miles inland along the old road to the coast, a road laid down on an early wagon track, which followed the Indian trace — a long day on sure feet giving way to oxcarts that took half the week to return from the sea with their burdens of salt hay. Now the coast is a scant hour's drive along Broadway, North Lowell Street, Main, and also River Road and Water Street, since the way sometimes skirts the muscular currents of the Merrimack, which salts at Newburyport, and pours into the Atlantic.

By the end of its journey the river is almost two hundred miles from the cold rose of its source in the White Mountains. In many places it flows through a yielding channel older than the ice ages. Where it courses over stubborn ledge, where the rock wears away at an incremental pace, are the waterfalls that were once the gathering places and fishing grounds of the Algonquin tribes. Merrimack is their word. River of sturgeon, swift water, strong place.

To the south of our fields and woods the river flows broad and braided and eastward. It is the strong line of our landscape. The low-lying hills slope towards its channel, and every vein of water — the icy melt and the murk, the mineral-rich source and the field-drained runoff, waters that taste like metal on the tongue, waters redolent of balsam, and some of smoky tea — every vein drains into the Merrimack. Even the cut of the road depends on the river, since it nearly ghosts the water's course though we sleep beyond earshot of a steady current, lulled instead by the fine-tuned motors of the night freight trucks that approach and then pass.

I
HOUSE

"BUILT BY a frugal man in a frugal time," my father likes to say of my house, and even now, when the plumbing or heating gives out, he'll mutter that it would have been cheaper simply to raze the place and build a new one. So many surfaces made level with shims, and supports that have had to be supported. Newspapers and *The Saturday Evening Post* pulled from gaps in the walls, and the back stoop propped up by loose bricks. When a robber kicked in the side door, and I came home to the September air swirling through the rooms, I found two rusted nails in the hingehole where one screw should have been. Such jerry-rigged things turn up as unexpectedly as Indian flints, and like those flints, I imagine I'll never stop finding them.

The frugal man was Ben Prentiss, and the time, about 1920, just after he had married Clara. He bought

3

two acres of land from my grandfather on what was then the edge of the farm, though by the time my father bought the house from Ben's oldest daughter, he had also bought up land to the east, and the two acres stood in the middle of our farm. Ben sited his house on a small rise near the road, which gave him a good view of all the surrounding acreage. It's the natural site for any house, even now, though it's a house no one would build these days. Half of it is a ramble of unheated storage rooms leaning down to the shed, and the hallways take up almost as much space as the six rooms I live in, rooms small enough to keep to their singular purpose. In the bedroom there's only enough space for the bed and dresser; the dining room, four chairs and a table; the study, my desk.

I easily take up the place myself, and I have trouble imagining how Ben, Clara, and their two daughters lived here, with the one closet, and even a slight cough carrying through all the rooms. The shallow well must have gone dry summer after summer. In my first years here — I had moved to this house when I returned to the farm to live — there were months when I couldn't water the garden and take a shower in the same day. The new driven well took no time at all to drill — an oversized rig backed in the driveway and bore through three hundred feet of ledge in a scant six hours. The source puts out so much water my brother Sam uses it to irrigate the tomatoes. Drawn out of the deep bedrock, clear, hard, cold, it courses through the skewed elbows of Ben's copper pipes — old pipes, still, and if I am away for a while the water comes up rust.

Of the grace Clara likely added to the house — the wallpaper streaming with flowers, the frilled curtains, the china cups — not a vestige remains, though much of what she planted in the yard still comes back every spring. She must have loved blues and purples — there are two islands of bearded irises among the meadow grasses, and violets spread under the west window. Lilacs bloom come May and soften the frame of the house — so upright, white, and unshuttered.

She had died, the two daughters had grown and moved on before I was born, so I have always called this house "Ben's house." As roaming children, in our boredom we would stray here. Most of what I remember now is a dark kitchen steeped in smoke and cooking oil. One of my cousins remembers shards of colored glass strewn on the floor of the shed. My sister, chickadees pecking at the sills where Ben left peanut butter for them. We all remember his pale, lank frame, and a fine nose with steel-rimmed glasses pinched on them. There were few words, though I don't think he was ever unwelcoming.

Most of the evidence of living was in the kitchen by then — the chair camped at the wood stove, and a table beside it with the day's paper, a flowered cup and plate, and a steel boning knife. The stove itself could be kept low since it only had to throw off enough heat to warm the one man rocking there. The quiet rush of fire contained in metal. No flame to draw his gaze. My mother would invite him for Sunday dinners, and sometimes he'd come, but only after long coaxing.

Dust in a slant of light. The grass springing back in his footfalls. Things that must have been stored in the shed while Clara had been living he had moved into the house — a good supply of cordwood, bundles of newspapers, empty bottles and cans. After her death he saved everything, right down to wood scraps and string. When he himself died, what his oldest daughter didn't take down to Virginia my father and uncles sorted and cleared away, and they ended up burning much of it on a windless spring morning in 1980.

What in these rooms would Ben and Clara remember as theirs? The plank of bird's-eye maple that runs half the length of the dining room floor — surely they'd know that — and the rough pine shelves in the kitchen, smoothed now from years of paint. But here is another life, with its own dishes, and no curtains, and a Turkish rug in the front room. The floorboards are sanded and glossy with urethane; the walls, painted a creamy white. On the fine shelves that must have held their keepsakes, my books are a square and solid weight. I think the place would be strange to them, they who had lived here so long their windowglass rippled like quiet water, and their view softened with the distortion.

It was a view that must have had its familiarities from the start — both Ben and Clara grew up nearby, and always lived bounded by the Merrimack to the south and the low hills to the north, mill cities to the east and west. At times I try to imagine this house containing a whole long life. It feels small when I think about it, confining, and sometimes comforting — as it would, I suppose, to anyone who has lived in more places than she ever could have imagined. I can't gather everything under one roof anymore. Not enough space, enough time, no way to close the distances between all the things I love.

Sometimes there's no sound where I think a sound should be. The air warms unexpectedly, a dense fog slips into the orchard behind the house, and my ears strain for the three foghorns — I used to count to eleven between them — warning down the bay. And then I think how I should be hearing the drawn-out cries of oceangoing birds, and smell salt on the thickened air, and my chest tightens. How far away they now feel, the old friends who are strangers to the slope of these hills, and the names on the nearby graves.

By the time I moved back to the farm, the windows in this house were shaky in their frames. The ropes on the lead weights had frayed, the glazing compound had gone dry. That first winter I listened to the glass knock against the wood on fierce nights, and to the reedy wind. I could feel the drafts in every room. As soon as the warm spring days came, I replaced all the old windows.

Now that the glass is new, the far hills don't shimmer through it, and the skies don't have their distortions — and they won't — not for another half-century at least. The glass is so clear, it sometimes feels as if there's nothing at all between me and what I look out on, which is our apples to the north, peaches to the south, a field of corn to the west, blueberries to the east. Or I read the compass again: my parents to the south, my aunt to the east, my brother to the west.

↗ ↗ ↗

When the irrigation pond turned the color of coffee, my father knew it had to do with the trench Gil Johnson had dug just to the west of our land. Runoff from the trench flowed into the brook, which in turn carried silt to the pond. My father knew this without ever seeing the trench or the runoff beyond his property. He was just used to the habits of the land. They were in his bones — the drainage patterns and the cold spots where frost lingered, and where the marginal soil was only good for a side crop of gourds. He knew it was nearly impossible to grow lima beans and that he'd sometimes lose his peach crop. It was the accumulation of his life-time and of his father's life, too.

All through the growing season, that accumulation was right in front of him. He couldn't move to the right or to the left of it. It told him when to irrigate, and when to harvest, and when to call it a loss. Even after the workday had ended it was there at the dinner table. "You should eat some tomatoes," he'd say, "they'll be gone in a few weeks, there's been so much rain." Or we'd be trying a new variety of corn: "Sweeter than Seneca Star," he'd say, to no one in particular. After dinner he'd tune in the weather one last time and doze in the easy chair until bedtime.

His longest days were during the months of August and September, and in an exhausted hour he'd wish he'd done something different with his life. His brothers had gone on to other occupations — electrician, teacher, contractor, mechanic — and their lives seemed buoyant in the world, designed orbits. And he: nothing other than his father's son.

But such regrets slowed as the season slowed. November came and the moon rose over bare maples. The boughs of the apple trees were sprung and still. Winter rye was up in the cornfields. Only cabbage and cauliflower remained standing — they could be picked even after the first frosts, and then the ground was too hard to turn over. My father had more energy in the longer evenings and began a book that would take him all winter to finish. He liked James Michener and would read *Alaska* one year and *The Caribbean* the next. He'd garner a handful of facts out of all the pages, and the more he read the less accurate was his recollection of those facts. What he brought to the dinner table was something half-recalled and misremembered. All the same, he relished such talk, as if he was just singing for the song, since the words weren't tied to silt or runoff or coffee-colored water, since for once his words flew away as he said them.

⚹ ⚹ ⚹

My mother's ear is tuned to the distance, to a hawk's cry — asthmatic, from out of the blue. Or the sound of someone driving a wedge into wood: *chink, chink, chink* for so long, then his arm must give a little since his aim falls off its mark and the sound off its pitch. Of course, there's the engine noise of a tractor making its way across one of the fields. A change in the engine marks a change in the land or the end of a furrow. And every day at noon the truck door yawns and snaps shut, then the door to the mudroom, and my father is there at the kitchen entrance. He scrubs his hands at the sink and turns on the TV to get the same weather he heard at breakfast. Then he turns down the volume on the set and lets the news run on while they have their lunch.

They eat at the kitchen now, sitting kitty-corner to each other at the small round table. They look at the salt, the pepper, the bread, the way in winter they'll look at the fire when they talk to each other. They talk about us children, of course, of money and errands to run, the health of their friends. There's silence, and sometimes one of the old stories.

In other years we ate lunch in the dining room or on the long porch table, since there were four kids and Pete, my father's right-hand man. My father and Pete had their own talk: codling moth, cultivator, rye spreader — they were going over the morning's work or mapping out the work still to be done in the day. There was some borer in the next piece of corn, the tomatoes needed water, the orchard should be mowed. My mother served lunch, and the conversation went on around her.

↗   ↗   ↗

She had never in her life made a pie, so those first Tuesdays of her marriage my mother would walk up the road to watch them bake in the farmhouse kitchen. She'd stand to the left of my grandmother and my aunt with her eyes fastened on their hands as they cut the lard into the flour. The steel tines of the pastry cutter were long off their gleam, and the wooden grip was every bit as smooth as the scythe's. Straight into the flour they'd cut, and then they'd give the bowl a quarter turn and cut again. Again, until all the fat had disappeared into the flour. "It should look like soft bread crumbs," they told her as they flecked the mixture with water. "And the water must be very cold, but don't use too much or the dough will be tough." "Don't handle the dough any more than you have to," they'd say, as they scraped the mixture up to form two rough cakes, which they let rest under a towel as they made the filling.

Since she was married in late spring, she learned first to make rhubarb pies. They didn't measure anything for the filling, but simply tossed in the sugar and spices and cornstarch. "When you roll out the crust don't use too much flour on the board." "Make sure it's not too thick, but don't roll it too thin." "And do it right the first time because it won't be flaky if you have to roll it out again."

In her own home, she added too little water at first, and the ball of dough crumbled under the weight of the rolling pin. She had to patch crusts. She had to finger them into the pans. She had to roll them out again. Filling seeped through the bottom crusts and spilled over into the oven. Late in the day all she could smell was sugar and fruit burning off the oven floor. She stared down the hours to dinner, stared down all the Wednesdays and Sundays to come. She stared down latticework crusts on the blueberry pies, the star of steam vents on the apple, the fluted edges of the squash pies, and the fork-tined edges of the mince. Easier to pass through the eye of a needle than to learn this.

A house settled. Lines no longer plumb to the design. I remember my mother working without falter. I see her scooping the flour from a canister and leveling the dry measure with a butter knife. She cuts in the shortening with quick, efficient strokes, and the water she uses is as cold as the brook that spangles my wrists when I plunge in my hands. To roll out the dough she rocks the pin on top of it at first and then works out from the center, giving each stroke even weight. She rolls away, then to her right, towards her, and to her left until she is north once more. She lifts and turns the dough, then follows the compass again, rolling in all the directions of the wind.

She'd make rhubarb pies first thing every spring, followed by sour cherry — until the birds got to the trees. Blueberry and peach ran down the summer and overlapped the first apple pies made with Gravensteins. She made one or two pies with McIntosh, and then worked with Cortlands. But as soon as the Northern Spies were ripe she used only them — so deep is their flavor — until the last punky ones were pulled from the apple cellar sometime in March. She'd make squash pies in the fall and winter, too, of Blue Hubbard and butternut.

She's making a Blue Hubbard pie today, and after forty years my father still doesn't know that she needs only two cups of cooked squash for the filling. He has brought her the heel of the largest seed squash of the season, which must weigh six or seven pounds, and she has to struggle to cut away its skin and cube the orange flesh. To the steamed, mashed squash she'll add milk, eggs, sugar, cinnamon, nutmeg, and also ginger. It will be the one pie she makes this week now that it's just the two of them, and she'll work slowly, since she's bothered by a little arthritis in her wrists.

⚡ ⚡ ⚡

It is early March. Old snow in the woods, and mornings, anyway, frozen ground. Just visible in the matted grass is a set of wheel ruts leading down to the orchard. My father has begun to prune the young apple trees — a stir at the edge of a long sleep, nothing more. Any spring snow will put an end even to this light work. But the good weather makes him want to start the season, and for now he thinks about pruning two rows every good morning. He can work from the ground, and the young trees go quickly. Each needs only a few cuts, where two branches cross each other, or where a secondary limb competes with the leader. And the branches are slender. A snip, or a few draws of the saw is all. He keeps a pruning hook in the bed of the pickup for the rare branch that's out of arm's reach.

It's the older trees that are a job of work. They were planted so long ago, some of them, not even he knows who first pruned them. Now they've grown almost too large to pick with ease, and to shape them means using ladders and crawling up their slant limbs. Now and again a chainsaw. And a long time spent deciding on which cuts to make. He has to prune around years of wind damage as well as the work others have done — some trees are as skewed as homes with seven previous owners.

But the best are a good part trunk. He likes their gray, bull-necked strength. And their turned grace — branches spare as antlers contain light and air even in the center of their crowns. They'd show the smallest neglect. He's seen whole hillsides let go — apple trees shaggy as hermits, branches turned in on themselves — a tangle of nests — or flung wide or strayed to the ground and flailing in the simplest wind.

Well, this morning's work has tired him more than he'd thought. The house feels overheated. Maybe a short doze . . . He hears my mother making lunch — no more than a pin falling — and now the morning's work seems far off in another country — like tomorrow's work . . . the work of sixty years . . . He sleeps the same as if he's seeded all the fields with hay. Just sweet hay.

✦   ✦   ✦

My brother Sam has lived here, only here, for more than half of any long life, and the land is still not his own — not his orchard, not his fields, not his to dream on, not his to lose. More than anyone, he's bounded by these stone walls, the pines, these furrows. And no one talks anymore as if there'll be another life for him. "Maybe Sam should have done something different," my mother says, "gone out on his own."

The corn snow draws back to the shadows, and the blue-eyed cold once more has lost its edge. My father finishes pruning the new orchard while fields away my brother burns piles of brush on top of sodden grass. Smudge casts off from his fires. It billows and drifts above the oaks, it smarts in his eyes and throat.

ʎ ʎ ʎ

The spots on the tomato leaves have them both stumped. I see them on opposite sides of a trellis, both bent to the foliage, lifting their heads to speak to one another or nodding in agreement. Sam rises and shows the underside of a leaf to my father, who takes it and turns to his left to see in better light. Another nod. It's clear the things they know wash over the same territory.

I don't often see them like this. Usually they keep to themselves. My brother is grading tomatoes or picking the day's corn while my father is checking the color on the apples or cultivating a late field. They agree before-hand that come September my father will oversee the apple picking; my brother, the squash harvest, so if my father mutters that too many of the Macs have dropped, Sam only says, "If it was up to me I'd have started picking them earlier." My father might answer back by saying something about there being no market for green apples. My brother shrugs, "Fine." And then there's silence.

I know Sam's head is full of ideas. We have a small orchard, harvested the same way it's been harvested all along. There are apple boxes so old the pine is splintering away from the nails. Bottoms give way, and thirty or forty pounds of fruit spill onto the concrete floor of the apple cellar. He has worked it all out on paper — a system with bins, and the forklift to go with it. He'll have to enlarge the door of the apple cellar, and grade the approach . . . He used to rattle off ideas like this, but these days he simply says, "Nobody does it this way anymore."

I know my father is silently running down all the projects Sam has left undone. The shed half shingled, one of the tractors disassembled . . . He is biting his tongue. It's been a long time since he's talked to someone about the day's work — what to pick where, or how it's still too wet to plow. Or told someone a little of what he knows — say, how best to graft the scion to a rootstock. How the cut has to be clean, and the cambium should match all the way around.

🙺   🙺   🙺

One winter, years ago, Sam went so far as to clean up one of the unused sheds and set up a carpentry shop: try squares and spirit-levels, chisels, gouges, planes, hammers, and saws; cherry, oak, and maple spaced and stacked to finish seasoning. Bright nails gleamed, and the air was sweet and thick with sawdust and the scent of fresh cuts — a promising fragrance above the must of old canvas and leather.

At the dinner table he would talk as if he was born to it. He'd talk about applied geometry and dovetailed joints, and how he was going to build a cabinet of cherrywood; the clean, broad planks cut easily into a roughed-out shape in his mind. Or he envisioned an oak desk worked from dimension timbers — ponderous oak, with the grain dreaming through it, which would deepen under his own hand as he rubbed oil into its surfaces.

For a while we believed he'd found his place at last, but such craftsmanship lives in the patience and work of real time — the same as this farm — and if his troubles have canceled out anything, they've canceled out an understanding of such time. He's used one drug or another for years, and by now his habit has settled into a rimey life of its own. He goes unwashed and unshaven, and his clothes are ragged. He is sullen and alone. I can imagine his night sweats, with his pillow and sheets soaked through, his eyes shining and feral.

It was no surprise when he began to spend less and less time in the space he'd cleared and set up, saying he was waiting for a certain tool he'd ordered, or for the wood to season a bit longer. And as always, he said, "If you're going to do it, you might as well do it right." And then: "You never think I can do anything right . . . You think I'm just a screw-up, go ahead and say it."

And sometimes I do. I say it when the apples are un-sprayed or the corn is late in getting planted. I say it when the crew is hanging around the packing shed waiting for him while he lies in bed dreaming of build-ing an addition to the farmstand or a new greenhouse in which to grow early tomatoes.

2

BACK

"I THOUGHT you were living off somewhere else," the customers at the farmstand will sometimes say. Or they ask, "What's brought you back?" I mention something about how the place is so much work now, or I talk about my parents being old.

When I ask it of myself, there's a winter's night I remember. It was before I returned here to live, and we were all home for Christmas. "I've never seen Sam looking so bad," my sister, down from New Hampshire, said. It was true, too, for as much as I could know. I was only living outside Boston, but I saw Sam about as rarely as my younger brother did, who was in from the West.

Sam lived then, as he still does, in a place stalled mid-renovation. We walked into a comfortless house, with insulation half-packed against the exposed two-byfours and a plywood floor with grime scuffed in. He'd drawn the shades against the daylight and had a few lamps on. I don't remember any color. A small engine taken apart in a corner of the living room. Empty take-out containers on the table. Coke cans. Candy wrappers. Cold.

My sister, my younger brother, and I sat there in our winter coats and tried to talk to him over the TV about the way his life was going. His eyes were sparks, and he himself, thin. His talk was all farm. We heard again how there was too much work here, never enough help. His hands were tied. Dad would never change anything. If we tried to turn the conversation towards his own life, towards his unpaid bills, the cocaine and mood swings, he'd ride over us and say, "You don't know. You're not around. You try working here for fifteen years." And then he'd get up and pace and spin off into some of his dreams. "I could do so much with this place — we should be planting the first corn under plastic. We could go into greenhouse tomatoes. It's early money — Dearborne makes a killing every spring. If I had some help, someone to run the stand . . ." We were sunk low in his couch and looking straight at him. He stopped pacing and, for a minute, there was silence. When he started up again he looked at each of us hard, and in turn, as he said, "You left. You left. You left."

My first season back I was stunned by the business, how it now takes four, sometimes five people to run the stand, and still, on Sunday mornings we can't pack the corn fast enough. We sell all we can possibly pick — at least one hundred bushels, and I hardly look up from my work as I answer the customers' questions: "The corn? We've had it for about a week now." "Yes, thirteen to a dozen — just like last year." "Bring the water to a boil, and cook it four to six minutes." "Four to six minutes — that's it."

When I was a child, and my father still sold most of what he grew to the neighborhood markets in Lawrence and Lowell, the farmstand was a three-sided shack, just one step up from a table on the lawn. It had built-in counters on each side. The left one was at a slant, with the corn piled on it; the right one, level and waist high to the customers, held tomato baskets full of beans, peppers, squash, and tomatoes. The strongbox was tucked in the back. The scale, with its round face and white enamel pan, hung from a crossbeam. Against the back wall, bushels of corn were stacked, and a grape box, hung as a shelf, held half a dozen jars of honey, which I'd arrange in a diamond pattern, then rearrange in straight rows, and again in staggered rows. The honey always stood in shadow, and seemed a solid chestnut color. Sometimes a scrutinizing customer would take a jar and hold it up in sunlight to check its clarity, and it turned to translucent amber.

I couldn't have been more than ten when I started to take my turn minding the stand. The midday shift went to the youngest because the road was quietest then. The

summer air: quiet, and hot, and bright. I remember
times when not one customer would come, though
mostly you could count on a trickle of people — many
older ones who would come for a few ears of corn, and
a pound of tomatoes:

"That tomato's not soft, is it?"

"No, sir."

"Are you sure you counted right?"

"Yes, sir."

"An extra one for me? That's a girl. How's your father? All right?"

"All right."

After they drove off, I could hear the car engine clear
to the bend in the road. Then, the quiet again. I'd tilt
my chair against the back wall, and draw the same scene
over and over again on the back of a No. 12 bag: the
view from the stand. In the foreground, a telephone
pole, the mailboxes, a clump of grasses spiked with
chicory. Across the road were the stone garage, the red
shed, fields, and woods.

When I went off to college, and afterwards lived
away, I remembered the stand as that same white, dusty
place, even as I heard how they were building the new
stand, which was closed in and at least a dozen times the
size of the old one. They bought a cash register and put
in a phone. They paved the parking lot. Sam hung a
carved sign by the side of the road, which had steadily
grown busier over the years as housing developments
sprang up, and the corner markets in the cities closed

down. He dragged the old stand behind the green-houses and used it as a place to store empty crates.

The feel, for instance, of a ripe ear of corn was something I'd never forgotten, or how to spot signs of borer, and the grade on the apples and tomatoes. Such things kept me in good stead when I returned, but it had been fifteen years, and there were many things I had to learn for the first time. I knew nothing about the wholesale orders or the preferences of the customers. I heard things like "Well, they always let me pick out my own corn" and "They used to save me the large zucchinis for my bread" and "Last year . . ." I was a stranger, too, among the others who work here now, among Sallie who seems to have been here forever, and David who'd tagged along beside my father since he was twelve, who'd taken over for his brother, who'd taken over for another brother before him. There were small, long-running jokes between them — just the way David said "beans" or "harrow" or "water" could make Sallie roll her eyes or laugh.

I don't even know when I could first discern David's forthright stride from across two fields, or when I could sense, without looking, Sallie's presence at the side door, and I'd know she was resting her brow against her knuckles as she leaned against the jamb. We'd count the days down by the varieties of corn — Sprite giving way to Seneca Brave, then to the slow-growing August varieties — Sweet Sal, Sweet Sue, Calico Bell. I'd lift a bushel onto the table and David would appear out of nowhere to help me lift it the rest of the way. Sallie, beside me, packed the dozens and half-dozens into the brown bags, and our small talk bloomed during some of the brief respites, then fell away. "Once you know this work," she'd tell me, "there's nothing else." I'd always agree with her, even if I haven't always believed it for myself.

And I no longer believe it for Sam. The talk between us is still that iron wheel — orphaned and unwieldy, and I'm always afraid it will run loose. I wonder at how I could have thought it would be weightless. I have a harder and harder time remembering the boy who built a treehouse in all his free time, his scrapwood steps nailed to the trunk of the specimen maple. I don't even know if it's a memory or a dream — him building his raft or his radio or leaning into his stride as he skates along the circumference of the pond. And what of five years back — all that I felt — where has it gone? — that winter's night, when it was me he turned to and said *You left.*

When I close the front doors of the stand at six there is a sudden, pronounced quiet. The bushel baskets, the bins, the cleared counters emanate a new coolness, as if I'd descended into a cellar. It's the first moment I've had to myself for at least ten hours, and I take a long breath. My own house is quieter still, and when I enter, it feels as if I had left it ages ago. I'm surprised by the scent of cut flowers — snapdragons, zinnias, bachelor's buttons — and by the sight of them in the vase near the window. I don't remember leaving the coffee cup on the counter after breakfast. Or the morning paper spread across the table. A lace curtain stirs. I can hear the clear, minor notes of a sparrow.

Corn husks rough up my hands just as much as sandpaper would, and the day's dirt lodges in the loosened skin. The first thing I do those evenings is soak and scrub my hands at the kitchen sink. It's an absent-minded task. I lean against a high stool and gaze down the orchard to the darkening pines. The water is lukewarm, nearly the same temperature as the air, so I can't really tell where one leaves off and the other begins. The sound of water falling back into water. The landscape disappearing into the soft night. Some evenings I am so long there that my fingerpads start to wrinkle. I dry my hands, then rub lotion into them.

✦ ✦ ✦

For half a dozen years I lived on an island thirty miles into the Atlantic. On a winter's night, the town was no more than one small, uncountable cluster of lights, tight as the Pleiades. The dark outer reaches, swept by the lights of three lighthouses, were hardly inhabited, and beyond, even darker, and everywhere, was the northern ocean. Milk, butter, eggs, the obedient cantatas practiced by a choir — in rough weather such things could seem miraculous.

It was like nothing I had ever known. Weather reports contained words that had hardly ever crossed my family's lips — buoy bell, moontide, small craft warnings, and moderate seas. Near gales — so different from our inland winds. There were plants and trees I had never seen: scrub oak, bayberry, sweetfern, and heath. Even the white pines — long familiar to me — grew there in unfamiliar ways. By rights I think of them as slender and straight, sistering the masts they were once felled for. There they are hardly taller than the houses, and their jagged crowns lean into the land as if the work of all their years was to endure winds coming off the entire compass.

When I think of the island now, I like to remember the shortening dusks of September and October when I'd walk to the end of the road to watch the full moon rise over the Atlantic. I'd shelter myself in a dune, with my back to moorland that had turned burgundy and rolled away like a sea of its own. The surf sounded innocent in the distance. An orange glint over the gray-green water, then the orange moon itself rose pale — nearly transparent — on the horizon. Warmer days I'd stay and watch it hang low there before making my way home in the dusk. On the road back the winterberries blazed out from their bark. The white trim of the summer houses — shuttered where they faced the sea — was luminous in the failing light.

The trim would shine, too, in my headlights on my early drive to work. I'd leave home a good hour before sun-up and drive the seven miles to town past sleeping houses lost in a land darker than the sky. Until their white paint came up in my lights, only their angled outlines distinguished them from the low woods and fields. It was close enough to morning so that the deer had begun to move, and clusters of them would appear in the middle of the road. As my car approached, they'd raise their heads, turn, and stare at me. I'd stop and shut down my lights, which would bring them to, and they'd look forward, then break into a run. A rustle of underbrush, a glimpse of their white flags going away, then they were gone.

At that hour there couldn't have been more than a handful of people awake — I'd count them to myself — the third shift at the power plant, the night officer at the police station, and the other bakers like myself. For the first several hours I worked alone making batches of bread and shaping the morning pastries. It was steady work at a long maple table, and small sounds told its rhythm: as I divided the risen dough into equal pieces, the dough cutter struck the wood regularly and with a dull thud. White, oatmeal, wheat. The cut dough sprang back into crazed shapes that gave under my touch as I'd knead one after the other into uniform smooth oblongs and set them in the black tin bread pans. Then I'd turn to the pastries, which required more painstaking work. It took the same kind of patience my mother had when she rolled her grape leaves. You had to find an efficient rhythm, but you couldn't rush. One after another of the almond pastries twisted into the same figure eights, cheese into spirals, cherries into circles, then set to rise in staggered rows on parchment.

The pastries would be in the oven and the bread well into its second rise when the first streaks of winter dawn appeared. If I had time, I'd stand out on the back stoop to finish my coffee while the sun came up over the bay. The long stretch and wake of the town had begun. As I looked down the slope to the water, I could see upstairs lights, and beyond, a dozen scallop boats making their steady way to the far reaches of the harbor. The drawn dredges like tucked wings, the fishermen stock still, one hand on their wheels, staring ahead. The small wake each boat made unfurled into others, and then attenuated into loose waves that lapped against the shore. I could see the early ferry easing out into open ocean. As it passed the jetties, the seals — indistinguishable from the granite at that hour — stirred, and slipped off the rocks into the water.

The life of the restaurant began to wake too. Steve, who cooked breakfast, stumbled in at the last possible minute, and within minutes after his arrival the smell of bacon frying overcame the aroma of the bread in the ovens. Onions and potatoes sizzled on the grill. His whisk slapped against the metal bowl as he made his pancake batter. Our talk. What we did yesterday, the boss, the customers.

And more conversations as the waitresses arrived to

set up the dining room. From back in the kitchen, we couldn't hear more than murmurs when they clutched around the coffee machine. Then they'd scatter to set up the tables, and their voices would grow louder as one would call across the dining room: "You *have* to tell him . . ." They'd meet again at the coffee machine to finish the story in voices low and intimate as if between sisters.

Once the customers arrived, the place was awash in voices. A dozen conversations among tables and between tables. Births, deaths, real estate, a story circulates. A death or a scandal could be all the talk in such a closed world the way one topic could have consumed days on the farm years ago. Something as small as honey. "Pop was always wishing for honey," my father has told me, "but we didn't have the money for it. Then a wild swarm landed in the Baldwin tree. What an event, when Pop captured that swarm. He took the gray mare and went to see Mrs. McLaughlin, who told him how to make a box for them. It was all we talked about for weeks. It kept him hoping for months. But the bees starved that winter, and we never did get any honey."

By the time I finished my shift it was broad day, and the life of the island was fully awake. With all the daily bustle it seemed so much less an island than when I first awoke. Always the night accented its tossed place on the sea. I clearly remember the evenings I went to gather a friend from choir practice. I could hear the music from streets away — interthreaded voices cast into the immense night, and thinning into the greater dark beyond us. The sung words I heard were the same simple old ones: *so that I may be a child of peace; and let me come to thee from my sorrows.* What made them complex was the steeped unity of the voices singing them. Our own comfort, they seemed to say, or none at all.

A comfort it was hard for me to conjure when the wind came out of the east — the same direction where that moon had so calmly risen. There were stories all over the island of people going mad from such wind. They would be found, the stories go, their fire gone out, sitting and staring into cold ash. I'd keep a fire going all the time on such nights, and sit right next to the flame. Sometimes I'd sleep the night beside it. Even so, there were times when the wind sounded so fierce — the brays, the creaks, my whole house sounding like something in the way — the fire couldn't calm me. In the end, I opened the door to find my peace. Outside, only the sound of pine boughs sweeping in that wind. The mist hid the cold gleam of the stars. Bare branches glistened in the glow of my houselights. By the time I was calm, my hair and face were soaked by a fine rain.

My father was always saying that island wasn't fit for a billy goat. He has lived all his years among the water-worn hills of this cultivated valley, a land shaped by hands and tools and machinery. Most of what we see here are the thought-out lines of our own making — wheel ruts, staked rows, stone walls, and the pliant trace of a furrow accommodating the rises and curves of the earth. Here, every inch has been built on, given up on, reclaimed and built on again. In the pathless woods you can read the history of European settlement — cellar-holes within shouting distance of each other, dry wells, metal dumps, and wild asparagus. He remembers when the road was one lane and unpaved, and when it took a team of oxen two days to reach the coast. He remembers the first airplane to fly overhead. Sometimes the memory of these things is more vivid than the words he still lives by — harrow, plow, seed, soil, frost.

While I lived on the island I returned to the farm maybe two or three times in a year, and with each visit my parents seemed to grow much older. Slow to get up from their chairs. Lost thoughts. I'd greet my mother at the far end of my ferry ride, and I'd see how her hair had grown so white, and my heart would sink when I noticed — we had been the same height for so long — how I was now inches above her.

Even with such moments, the farm felt well in the past to me. And the distance seemed to widen more every time my father or mother — they had both lived with their own parents until the day they married — would suggest I come back, or my mother would ask, "Why are you living there?"

I was never able to say. I went to the island to live after I finished college — because I had friends there — only meaning to stay for a little while, the summer, maybe into the fall — until I decided what I would do with my life. I hardly imagined I'd stay for years.

So small and exposed, seven miles wide, fifteen miles

long. I don't know if I'll ever live in a place again where there's terror and beauty in such measure. I missed it for the longest time after I left, but it has been more than ten years now, and when I return for visits, even my longing for it seems remote, though sometimes I wish I could just take a walk along those dirt roads that score the moorland there. I used to walk the same way again and again — a hundred times — and then one ordinary day an arrowhead would turn up at my feet — its honed edge or its worked shape would catch my eye. The rains, they say, washed them onto the roads. Anyway, they were a wonder to find. When I moved outside of Boston, I ranged them on the varnished sill of my bedroom windows. Against the polish of that wood, and the mild sounds of traffic, they seemed only foreign and rough, and no more than curiosities.

I couldn't have moved to a more different world. My city neighborhood was a sturdy one, built up sometime between the world wars and ambling down just a bit since. Streetlights and houselights burned bright enough to obscure the night sky — a complacent sky, milky almost, the color of a pigeon's throat. Away from the salt-laden air, it was hard to get enough of my own breath. And a sheltered grace seemed to weigh down on me — those beautiful shade trees, straight and wide-crowned, arcing over the streets and the small yards. Even so, it was a world I longed to fall in with. If I were asked finally why I left the island I'd have answered it was just too small, and far. Now I had a commute to work with everyone else, though among so many strangers, I couldn't comprehend the years and effort it would take to feel as if there were familiar faces around me.

I'd see my family more often — the farm was only thirty miles away. When help was short I'd lend a hand on the farmstand or with the greenhouses, and what had touched me only for a moment when there was a sea between us — my mother's stoop, my brother's rough face — gradually became my cares. *If I had some help* . . . My father owned Ben's house by then, and when the old tenant died I moved in. Sometimes it's seemed a last resort. And more than once, especially of late, a thieving choice.

My mother and I are preparing a Sunday dinner. From my place at the stove I hear her setting the dining room table, and after she finishes placing the silverware beside the plates she moves around the dining room patting things, putting the slightest skewed things straight. Sam comes in, and she asks, "Why don't you wash up for dinner — comb your hair." He smirks and walks past her. The days he does give in, she seems so happy, happy with any little inch he will give, the smallest thing parceled out.

I hear Sam in the living room talking to my father about the plowing: "We're ahead this year — I'll have the plowing done by June." He sounds assured as always, and none of us says anything, though we know it's not true. Yes, the times he works long into the dusk tug at me for more faith. But my faith even in those good days has started to falter.

Sam's talk dominates the meal. Sometimes my father says a thing or two, but I know he is holding back what he really thinks for the sake of peace. I've grown as silent as my mother, and excuse myself after I finish the dishes by saying, "I have things to do."

I drive nearly an hour to the coast and walk for miles along the waterline. An expanse of sky, the slow lap of a calm sea. Far out, broken touches of white surf. Of course I try to imagine what my life would be like if I hadn't returned. The possibilities turning over in my mind, turning weightless and slow as a tethered astronaut. What kind of work would have filled the years? Would I have a family of my own? Where to from here? Could I live here and not be part of the work? From my dining room table or my study window, almost all of the farm falls within my view. Just a quick glimpse and I know it's Sam's blue truck trundling down the edge of the berry field. There are sounds I always hear: the steady progression of the mower, the jangling harrow, and the high-pitched fan of the orchard sprayer. And silence too often means the work's not getting done.

When occasional terns stray inland on the last reaches of an ocean wind, my father simply sees the same white birds that he has seen for eighty years. Birds he knows from here and nowhere else. They eddy over the fields, higher than the hawks, glinting and white as salt itself. If I see them when I'm especially tired, I'm likely to slip into a dream of that island where terns are countless among other birds we never see here — shearwaters, oldsquaws, cormorants, and grebes — birds whose names are part of a vocabulary that can't help me here. I should be concentrating on the words at hand: harrow, plow, seed, soil, frost.

3

IN SEASON

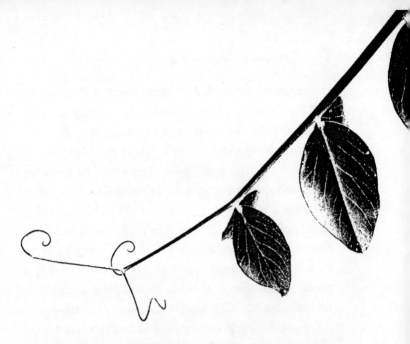

LAST NOVEMBER a night wind tore the plastic sheathing from the ribs of the greenhouse, and the exposed frame became one more stark contour in a land of bare trees and empty fields. The inside froze and filled with snow. Now, after a month of melt and spring mud, I can walk through what remains. The ribs still arch strong above me. Below, watering cans and plastic trays are strewn across the benches and floor. A stack of four-inch pots lists next to a heap of potting mix. There's a stray nozzle, baskets and hoes that belong in the shed, and an uncoiled hose. It looks as if a night wind had also torn through the inside, or as if we'd fled — from what? — overturning everything on the way out. But it's only that we have never taken the time to clean up.

I have registered so many winter months since, so much orderly time, that it's hard for me to comprehend the summer rush now. The mess seems only senseless, and I want to set it right, to check the hose for leaks, to rinse the pots, and wash down the benches.

It's more work than I think, taking me a long day to sort through the pots, discarding much and rinsing every salvaged thing with a weak solution of bleach. It takes even longer for my father and brother to raise a new roof over the old ribs. The poly is light but cumbersome to draw up and over the frame, and it's subject to the smallest breeze until it's secured to the wood and metal. Once that roof is on, though, the greenhouse feels almost new. If I stand in its center, the shapes and colors of the world outside — seen through translucent plastic — seem to be muted versions of themselves. It's warmer inside than out, and I can no longer smell the spring thaw — soft air, sap, the pliant earth — for the peat.

The day begins with a flat of tomato seedlings that need to be transplanted into pots of their own. I break open a bale of potting mix — closer to chaff than to soil it's so light — and fill each pot nearly to its rim. It takes a long time to saturate the pots with water, so I pass over the pots again and again with a running hose until they finally take on water, becoming dark and nearly faithful to earth. I make a hole in the center of each pot, then pull a seedling from the flat. Each one has already sprouted a set of true leaves beneath the growing tip, yet the entire seedling is hardly longer than half my little finger. I never feel my bulk so much as now, bent over these small starts with a wisp of a seedling grasped between my forefinger and my thumb. It would take no effort at all to bruise the cells in those stems, and I have to transplant five hundred of them.

By the end of the morning the greenhouse once again seems as it should, with filled pots spread across the benches, and the air warm and humid. It is a day without wind in the spring of the year. The roof above me is hardly measurable it's so thin — a frame for the ephemeral, made half of work, half of dream, sited, squared-off, saying *here*. Here is your house built nearly of air.

⚹ ⚹ ⚹

A sweet afterthought of a crop, these five rows of Knight peas that no one has had time to trellis amid the toll of June work. Now each row is a tangle of vines, leaves, tendrils, pods, and blossoms. To spot-pick the rows, Sallie and I have to pull back the whole green confusion. We can't tell which peas are ready for harvest by sight alone, since the pods are often blown full before the peas have ripened. We feel along the pod for the certain curve of a mature seed, or discern an incremental increase in weight. Slow-going, two-handed hours, and all through the first morning we check ourselves by shelling a pea now and again — they never taste sweeter than amidst those tangled rows under a long morning sun. There's no keeping them, really, since once off the vine their sugars turn to laden starch.

Seeded in cold ground and thriving only in a cool season, peas are among the first of the crops to ripen. It is late June, and there may be raspberries, too, in an early year, along with lettuce, say, and cucumbers. A small start, but enough of one to open the doors of the stand. Ours is broad and beamy and, at first, as orderly as whitewash: a scrubbed, granite-cool interior, over-wintered, empty, and full of shelf space. Is there a scent? A rub of resin, maybe the fragrance of milled pine, but nothing that speaks of time or history the way the barn does with its long-stored leather harnesses reeking of must, and all the laid-aside hoes and scythes, their hafts salted and polished by labor, their blades rusted, honed, and rusted once more. It's daunting, the thought of fill-ing all the unstoried space — these first tentative side crops hardly take up a corner, and when familiar voices break out of a seven-month silence, I believe I hear an echo:

"I've been watching the corn."

"Been waiting for you to open."

"Have a good winter?"

"Yes, yes, and you?"

Those five rows of peas are never again what they were during the first days of picking. Sallie and I spread blight with our boots and hands as we work over the rows, and we scar the undeveloped pods as we search among vines whose leaves have begun to yellow and curl. That single planting of peas is spent and harrowed down even before the first corn has ripened, and in some years the land is replanted with a late crop of car-rots or beans.

People are always saying that they haven't had their fill of peas, that we really ought to grow more of them, but in truth they soon forget about them once all the other crops begin to ripen: the early corn is also sweet, and there are tangled heaps of green beans and translucent wax beans that some still call butter beans; summer squashes warm from the field; beets and carrots pulled from cool, mineral earth; the spines of cucumbers and all the lettuces — Romaine and Boston and Red Leaf. Green onions, bunched radishes, and amber, hive-shaped jars of honey. Astringent thyme and parsley, basil, tarragon, wild marjoram, the mints. There's hardly any shelf space left in the last days of July. Even so, there are some who run ahead to a later season, some who have been dreaming of tomatoes for months and are impatient with the pink star at the blossom end of a stubborn green fruit. They ask after peaches as well, and pears and butternuts.

Now there is much talk happening at once, and conversations begin in midstream as if I was already familiar with the story:

"Those berries are for my son, you know he still can't leave the house."

"We'd be up to camp by now but she has her treatments."

"That's it, Kentucky Wonders — does anyone grow Kentucky Wonders? At the Center Street house my mother set them against the white fence . . ."

I can't follow the voices talking themselves into Au-

gust, when we can no longer keep up with all the ripe tomatoes and another scent has insinuated itself. What is
it? Something deep-seated — wild slip-skinned grapes,
I think, or apples bruised by a picker's thumb. I hear
flock-notes, and dusk is earlier by an hour. Half the
corn has been harvested. It never ceases now, the sound
of the disk harrow going over the old fields. A boy of
sixteen spends his days perched on a tractor, sitting
straight-backed as the one just man, breaking up the
straw-colored stalks of corn, and breaking them up
again.

⌁ ⌁ ⌁

In mid-July, green washes the landscape. Along the
brook bed, brambles and swamp maples. Lone pines,
deciduous woods, the soft contours of the cornfields —
not one yet plowed under. Summer runs down from the
day they start to pick corn. By 6:00 A.M. half a dozen
men are in the fields, dressed in oilers if the dew is
heavy. They work between the rows, snapping the ears
off and tossing them onto the flatbed, which hauls along
beside. My brother drives the flatbed and knocks down
the spent stalks as he goes. The corn is so high it hides
everything — the pickers, the truck, my brother — and
at some distances all I can see are ears of corn — ten or
twelve at a time — arcing over the stalks as the men
throw them onto the truck.

When I was growing up, for two solid months we'd
have corn for lunch and dinner. My mother put the

water on to boil while my father headed for one of the nearly ripe fields. He was checking to see if the corn was ready to pick, and he'd scour that field for a dozen ears ripe enough for us to eat. If it was a new variety he'd ask us what we thought. Wasn't it sweeter than Harmony? Didn't it have more flavor than Seneca Star? In truth we liked the squat, bright, early varieties the same as some slender, tapered ear with kernels tiny as milkteeth.

It didn't really matter, though, what we thought. To my father, the measure of all corn is Gold Cup, hardy and sweet, though each year he grows less and less of it because people clamor for bicolored corn now. Butter and Sugar the customers call it, or Honey and Milk.

♪　♪　♪

The varieties of peaches that grow in this part of the country have hardiness bred into them. Reliance. Elberta. Not names to dream on, though to grow peaches here, near the northern limit of their range, is something of a dream. My father was well over sixty when he planted the peach orchard in a longtime meadow. That was the last piece of land to be hayed — cut and cured and stored. I barely remember it, the rectangular bales spaced like footsteps across the land.

The peach trees — fifty or so of them — were no more than whips to start with, and it hardly seemed they'd survive a January. In truth, the trees don't always winter well — some years there is barely a crop and, once in a while, no crop at all. The peach orchard blooms early and pink. It will never look as crabbed and thickened with the years as an apple orchard — the trees aren't long-lived and they are pruned in their own way — without a central leader — so the limbs curve out and up to embrace an open center. Each crown, a ball-room of its own.

I have never seen relic peach trees crowding a cellar-hole the way apple trees often do. Apples are old in these parts, a cash crop talked about endlessly. How many times have I heard about the Ben Davis, no good for eating, that would cling to the branches until spring. About the long search for a McIntosh that would redden on the tree. Or the original Red Delicious fenced and locked at Stark nurseries. About cider years. Snow apples. Astrakhans.

Somewhere to the south there must be like stories about peaches. People traveling up from Georgia or the Carolinas will say our peaches just don't have the flavor of theirs. They'll name varieties I've never heard of that ripen right down the summer. Here the peach season doesn't last long — a few weeks in August and maybe the first of September when we have a fruit that isn't meant for storage, that doesn't smell sharp as the cold side of the mountain, and whose flavor isn't deepened by the frost. Reliance and Elberta are hardy names but, like all peaches, their fragrance blooms at the back of your throat as it passes.

⚹ ⚹ ⚹

Sallie still moves easily although she is well over seventy. Both her hands work the bushes, snapping the beans from the stalks and filling basket after basket. Now and again she might stand to stretch her back or rest her eyes on a stark, distant object — a lone gap-crowned pine or the white gate at the edge of the woods. Otherwise, on any good day, she keeps a level pace.

She won't work the bean field when it's wet — handling the crop then could spread rust — and she might quit early in too much heat. Sometimes the heat or constant rains drive two plantings of beans together. Then she can't keep up with them — no one can — and at last the earlier planting, mealy and tough, will have to be abandoned for the sake of the later one.

Sallie has worked outside so many years you can't see her sister in her anymore. Sometimes she'll drive the tractor if need be, or help when the tomato crop starts to get away. But mostly she keeps with the beans, accumulating bushels in some shade at the edge of the rows where my father collects them at the end of his day. And she'll mark tomorrow's place with a stack of empty baskets overturned against the chance of rain.

↙ ↙ ↙

Everyone has been wondering who'll pick the blueberries this year. Betty died over the winter, of a stroke, and the berries had been her job for nearly a dozen years. The ten weeks of a good berry season — July into

September — was just enough for her. She had come here in her retirement, as Sallie had, for some seasonal money, maybe a shape to the day.

During the peak weeks in August my father would send the newest, youngest help down to the berry field to help her out. "Pick where Betty tells you to," he'd instruct the boy as he fitted a coffee can with a make-shift neck strap, and the boy would lope through the apple orchard to the berry bushes happy to think that, at least for the day, there was no stooping, no dust, no cornhusks. He'd come back to the stand hours later dazed and sullen. "She kept after me like my own mother about twigs and leaves in my bucket," he'd say, and describe how she nearly stood over him to make sure he didn't pick anything green, and picked every bush clean. And he'd walk away muttering that he'd rather pick corn.

Well, it had come to be her berry field. She, herself, was meticulous and proud about the way she picked the berries. It seemed she barely touched them as they tumbled into the can. She would already be at work when I woke at six — she liked to start just as soon as it was light enough to see, and many days she'd have picked her sixty quarts by noon. I could see her white hat inching along above the bushes. Her filled buckets were covered with towels and set under the bumper of her car where it was cool — there every morning of every day in the slightest hint of dawn just as the first heat settled on the night-freshened grass.

Most likely the berry-picking will be shared among several people now. The payroll can run to eight or nine at the heart of the summer. Some have been here for as long as Betty, others skate along the surface for a few weeks, maybe for the apple crop, or for the September work. September can be difficult because there's still so much to do, and the high school and college students have gone back to their classes. Over the years there have been many who've started to work here at thirteen or fourteen and worked summers all during high school, and if they went to college, during college — moving irrigation pipe, picking corn, hoeing. My father has run through whole families of boys. When one grows old enough to move on to a job beyond the farm, his younger brother takes over. They still come around to pick up some corn at the stand and to say hello now and again. Richards. Davidson. Stark. By now some are middle-aged, and have grown children of their own.

The boys work the summers alongside two or three older men who begin the year with short days in March — pruning, tending the greenhouses — and stay on through the last trickle of work in November — cleaning up and grading apples for wholesale. Years ago, the full-time men came from town, but these days most residents are skilled or professional, and work elsewhere. Many who work here now were born in Puerto Rico or the Dominican Republic, and live in Lawrence. The radio in the packing shed is tuned to the Spanish station. Men who've worked in fields all their lives — outside of San Juan, and then in Texas, New Jersey, Florida. Roberto, who has been here seven years, is always remembering picking berries in New Jersey, or tomatoes, or zucchini. And, here or elsewhere, it's not likely his work will be different in the future.

Every April, as soon as things start to stir — Sam out working on the harrow, the shed doors open — sedans full of men pull in. One does all the talking, saying they know the work, they have a car, they can be here at seven every day. They'll work on Sundays. Sometimes a priest will come by with a man who knows no English at all, and so speaks for him. "He's a good man, and dependable. He's in church every week."

"We really have all the help we need."

"He has six children . . ."

We never had this much help when I was a child — the stand was much smaller, and we didn't grow such a wide variety of crops. I only really remember Pete. He had come down from Nova Scotia for work, and he came to the farm after losing three fingers in a cannery accident. He hoed, harrowed, planted — the same as my father — and as no one had before or since, he'd eat lunch with us. Every summer of my childhood he sat across from me on the porch table, his head dipping to half meet the plate with every bite. He ate steadily until he had cleaned his plate twice, hardly talking except to thank my mother, or to say "no thank you" when she offered him eggplant.

Pete passed away years ago, in his old age, during the clear, windless days of a January cold snap. Coming back from his woodpile he lost his footing on some ice, knocked his head against the frozen ground, and lost consciousness. An armload of split maple scattered around him. No one passing had seen him lying there in the yard behind his four-room house by the Merrimack. The short day slipped into night, and he died of exposure.

✤ ✤ ✤

As a child I'd wake on hot and clear July days to my father calling my brother from the bottom of the stairs. At 6:00: "Sam, time to get up." At 6:20: "Are you going to sleep all day?" At 6:30 my mother would begin to call — just his name — and after he eventually got out of bed he'd have to catch up with the crew in the cornfield.

Twenty years later, it's me who is calling him to work. I can't get into his house since the path to the kitchen door is grown over, and he took out the front door years back and walled in and shingled over the gaping space. The mailbox, once hit by a skidding car, has never been set right. He rarely answers his phone. My friend tries to tell me there are people like him all over New England. I don't think he ever goes anywhere. His truck is always in the yard, and at night his windows are dark. All I know for sure is that, somewhere far inside, the TV's on.

It's well past seven in the morning. I drive up the road

to his house in a fury, and punch on the car horn — short beeps at first. When that doesn't work I lean into it with all my strength. Sometimes his confused face appears in the bedroom window, and I drive off, knowing he'll shamble down to work in fifteen minutes or so. Other times, the more I lean on the horn, the more deeply he pretends to sleep.

⚹ ⚹ ⚹

His old friends ask after him. "I haven't seen Sam in a long time," they'll say. "Tell him to give me a call."

"I'll tell him you were by the stand," I say, "but, you know, he doesn't get out much these days."

If I'm grading tomatoes as I talk to them, I'll gesture at the work I have left to do, as if to suggest we're all strapped for time. They nod. They know the real reasons they don't hear from him, but let my brief reply stand in for everything that's wrong. Otherwise, where would I begin? Sam's troubles have become lived-in, as lived-in as the way my mother worries how he'll look each day: when will she see him, and what will his mood be like? Holidays, weekends, and workdays the same, winter, spring — she's waiting for his good days.

Lived-in, too, are the arguments between my father and brother. I have seen it so many times: my father behind the steering wheel of the truck, my brother on the outside braced against the driver's side door. My father's voice strains to keep in the anger: "You don't know how to order seed. Christ, this is enough tomato seed for five years."

"We need to plant more tomatoes this year."

"And who the hell's going to trellis and sucker them all?"

"If you'd hire more help . . ."

"If you'd get up in the morning . . ."

Perseverance is built into the work. It's one of the reasons I love the long rows of tomatoes to be trellised and the flats of seedlings to be planted. I love the patience it takes, the repetition, the deliberate pace, the way under the June sky, everything has to be handled just so; how it's always the same earth under my feet and that the tasks hardly differ from year to year, except maybe now there's an improved variety of corn, or the disks on the harrow are made of a more durable metal. But perseverance can't make up for everything, say, for the insufficient time I have to learn what I need to know about the late land and the cold spots. My parents are already old, and I came back late.

When Sam said he couldn't handle it on his own, did I really think he was talking about the greenhouse and the transplants, or pruning the tomatoes — those things that can be learned just by looking straight at them? I spend so much time on such things, on learning a knot sturdy enough to hold the late vines and simple enough to fall away after a frost. I make the days long and many and filled with work, and in August, if I finally break down at the end of a day, just break down, everyone can tell me I'm working too hard.

But it's not the work, the way it's not anything that perseverance can help. What can help if I'm simply afraid of my brother's exhausted face, afraid of what makes him so late and so sullen? What, when I can't remember a word between us that hasn't been misunderstood? Yes, there are times when he'll sit down and join in the talk about the spring planting or the apple crop. At such times that talk comes easier to him than it ever will to me. He's the one who learned early on about the cold spots and the late land and where the carrots should be planted. On those good days you'd swear he could take apart an engine and put it back again.

But even then, the distance between us is as small as my glance away when he looks at me, and as infinite. It's his eyes I'm most afraid of. When they have that cornered look and are glassy they're as incomprehensible to me as the spaces between the stars, spaces compelling me to stand fast and stare or else become a lesser creature.

≁ ≁ ≁

In a dry August, after the first piece of corn is plowed under, the field turns to a bald patch of rocks, rough clumps of soil, and wheat-colored stubble. The first piece of corn is almost always in the east field, and when that corn goes down, I can see clear across to the purple loosestrife that mats the swale around our irrigation pond. Loosestrife lines the brook bank, too. *Millweed*, my mother says, and tells me the seed had come here

snagged on raw wool from Europe. It worked itself
down the Merrimack from the textile mills in Lowell,
and took hold on the river's wide-curved banks, then
along its tributaries, then along every leaky little
stream and wash and pond in our parts.

Dry years it thrives the same as wet years: narrow as
candles, the spires of countless petals grow so close together they seem one — a fray of magenta in all the low
places. Everything else in the fields and woods is paled
by drought. A white haze hangs like mull over the land.
A man hitching down a weedy row, heat bugs searing,
the pickup trailing dust. You can't see the pond for
those weeds — they're tall as a grown child sometimes.

↙ ↙ ↙

Older people still say "drouth." They remember the
rasp of sere grasses and one bird's thin cry. They remember the plow scoring parched soils and a whole
season of crop loss. The corn stunted and dry-tipped;
the lettuce, bitter. Bitter the stem ends of the cucumbers. A season begun under such stress will never fully
recover, and so the late tomatoes were tough-skinned,
and the peaches so small they'd nestle in a young girl's
palm. What could they do to feel a little less like clay?
When they needed rain, the joke goes, they'd cut hay.

I say "drought," and I've always heard an engine in
the distance along with the tick of the irrigation nozzles
as the water turns in slow enormous arcs over the crops.
Water measured in hours and inches, and falling with

precise intensity on the corn and beans and tomatoes. Water that smells of iron and musk, and always enough as long as there's enough labor.

The irrigation pipe is moved by hand and laid down between the rows. When one field is watered for several hours, the pipe is moved to another, and after everything has had its inch, it's time to begin again. "That storm saved me a thousand dollars," I've heard my father say in the aftermath of a good rain.

This summer has been so dry that the west pond has been pumped down to the lowest level anyone can remember. It's all we seem to talk about: "Have you seen the pond?"

"No more than a few feet deep in the middle now."

"I know. Christ."

Field grass has taken hold on the banks, and three drums from a raft broken up in my childhood are at last exposed. There's an old lawnmower, too, and the remnants of some apple crates. Frogs squat along the edge, but the water has sunk below its inflow and outflow, so now it's too warm for the fish, and the heron is usually absent.

↗   ↗   ↗

Always that frail, white-haired woman, when she comes to the stand, rubs a leaf between her thumb and index finger and lingers over the fragrance of mint. Mrs. Mansur buys three bunches of flat-leaf parsley for her tabbouleh, and all the Italians, a sprig or two of basil for their sauce. Occasionally someone buys thyme or tar-

ragon but, for herbs, there isn't much more demand
than that. At most, they're a grace note, not a tried
thing to most of the customers — even the old ones.
And unlike the fruits and vegetables we grow, they
don't often work their way into the talk among neighbors here, which goes on all day long:

". . . Ned's not doing too well."

"That's too bad."

"Bill and I went to see him yesterday. He was pretty
confused. Wanted to come home with us, but I don't
know if he'll ever make it home again."

"You never know. Look at the Judge."

"You're right. You're right."

"George says the relatives are already coming out of
the woodwork."

"Always the way. What have you got there — tomatoes? They look good, I should pick some up — I was
just coming in for corn — the kids want a cookout . . ."

Corn, tomatoes, beans — everyone buys them without a second thought, but in the corner where the herbs
are displayed a grown daughter and her mother stop,
puzzled:

"Ma, what's this?"

"That's the thyme, I think."

Or a woman wonders aloud: "Tarragon. What would
you do with tarragon?"

"Some people put it in their salad dressing," I answer, "or you can try cooking it with chicken — it has a
little bit of a licorice flavor."

She crinkles her nose. "Chicken . . . Really?" her

voice having grown softer as she drifts off toward the summer squashes.

I imagine she's weary of cooking — like my mother — preparing the same few things the same way through all the years of her marriage. An arrow-straight task to get through the three meals she prays will yield no surprises and no complaints, and won't make too much of a mess to clean up. Tarragon. She'd wonder how much to use or when to add it in. And for what? For her husband to ask, "What have you put in this?" and then eat around it. And the kids. There they'd be, leaning their chins into their palms as they scraped all the green bits off to the sides of their plates.

We've only grown herbs for a few years, and I've always been the one to plant and take care of them. The seedlings are so small I don't even need a trowel — it's easy enough to push aside a bit of the fine tilth, place in the seedling, then tamp the soil back in. I set them along a white string, which keeps the rows straight, and then water them in. Most herbs don't attract pests, so they don't require much care except to keep them weeded and watered, and of course to keep on top of the harvest, since once they blossom, their strength goes into the flowers, and the flavor of the leaves is lost, or becomes bitter.

And though they are the least in demand of anything we sell, I give the herbs one of the best spots on the stand. Both my father and Sam shake their heads, and mumble under their breath, "You should be putting the cucumbers there." "All that space — and there's no money in it." I take far too much time with them, too, picking them myself every morning. Parsley, basil, chives, mint, tarragon, thyme. Each treated just a little differently. I shear off the parsley near its base so the new growth will come in evenly, and snip the basil just above its lower leaves. The perennial herbs are slower to grow, so I trim each plant sprig by sprig and bunch them in arbitrary sizes as I go — if there's plenty the bunches are big, if not . . . Each bunch sits in its own pint canning jar half full of water — a dozen or so jars in the coolest of corners, which only gets some western exposure. On a clear afternoon the water in the jars glints and there are skeins of sunlight on the leaves.

I know we are a long way from the old herbals I love to read, which tell me parsley sprung from the blood of a Greek hero, that thyme will keep up courage, and tarragon will cure the sting of a venomous reptile. Tinctures, tisanes, auguries. Vinegars, juleps, conserves, something for the cranial nerves. A pink bloom will decoct to a balm for a tired heart, and a deeply lobed leaf will recreate the eyes. In those books, something as small as a sprig of rosemary has the power to strengthen memory, and flourishes only in the gardens of the righteous.

What we have in these years is pure fragrance. Late in the day, a middle-aged man stops at the door of the stand. It's been humid lately, and sweat stains the back of his workshirt. His boots are unlaced to finally let in some air. He rubs his brow as he tries to remember what it is he's supposed to pick up for supper. I hear a long drawn-out breath, then he turns single-mindedly towards the wax beans. As he passes the herbs, I see him brush against a bunch of basil, enough so its scent quivers into the air. I can smell it too. He has stopped still — I don't think he's sure of what it is, though the more the scent diminishes, the more he seems to strain to know it, as I myself have strained to hear a note sustained after the bow lifts from the strings.

♪ ♪ ♪

Grapes have always grown wild here. The vines tumble along the stone walls and the old mail road, whose faint wheeltracks I can still follow through the back woods. Sometimes they climb the trunks of the white pines and curl along their lower branches, then cascade back down in a freefall, but mostly they grow back in on themselves, twining among brambles, bark, and stone so densely I can't see my way through them except for where a few stray tendrils curl away from the thick of it.

The vines are too entwined to produce any quantity of fruit, and what fruit there is ripens unevenly, so that one grape tastes sweet, and the next, bitter. But the smell is so musky, and the late summer air so deep with it, it stops me still, and I breach the tangle of vines — so strong it's like working against a floodtide. All that redolence, and so little fruit — a few small grapes is all I ever find to eat — way in — in clusters of three or four.

Years ago, my father dug up some of the better grape-vines from the mail road, and planted and trellised them alongside the farmhouse. He pruned them back, and he still prunes them every spring — you can see how severely in winter when, even with a season's re-growth, the vines sinew sparely along the wires and stakes. They remind me of flung arms, and I can see how they strain against their form — there are places where the vines perceptibly curve away from the wires then are reined back in again. Some braid around each other, and only a few tendrils and tips stray away. In late summer the fruit hangs in heavy clusters, and they're the grapes my mother has always used to make her jelly.

She picks them when they are still a little under-ripe — there's more pectin in them then — so the jelly will set more firmly. I can easily conjure her at the kitchen table picking through the fruit, discarding any that are bruised or too soft, and removing all the stems. She boils them in a stock pot, and within minutes the grape scent thickens, the kitchen suddenly as heady with it as that low place on the mail road. It is high sum-mer and the air doesn't move even with the windows thrown open. Her forehead is damp, her hair curls with the steam. The metal spoon is stained purple and lies on the stovetop, whose white enamel is splattered with purple, too.

As is the bleached cheesecloth she uses to strain the cooked fruit. The cloth catches all the skins and seed, and what passes through — juice the color of a dark gem — she returns to the pan along with sugar, and boils again. After awhile she begins to test the jelly for firmness by lifting the spoon from the pot and letting the mixture fall off its side. It falls first in two distinct streams. She dips the spoon and lets fall again, and again, until the streams sheet together and fall in unison from the middle of the spoon, which means the jelly is done. She skims the pot, then pours the mixture into six-ounce jars, which she seals with paraffin. Next day she caps the jars. A few she gives away, but most she stores to have with their breakfast all winter long.

In June, long before the first scent of grapes infuses the air, when the leaves on the vines have just unfurled and are still a bright green, and the fruit just hard green promises of themselves, my mother picks grape leaves. There are only a few weeks in the year when the leaves are tender and insect damage hasn't yet set in. She likes to walk along the mail road and pick from the wild vines. There are countless ones to choose from in the mass and tangle, but she picks carefully so they'll be of a uniform size, and not too deeply lobed. She cuts their stems as she picks them so they won't pierce the other leaves.

These she stuffs with a mixture of lamb and rice. She places some filling near the base of the underside of the leaf, and tucks in the sides as she rolls it towards its tip. She rolls them firmly enough so they won't fall apart during their long cooking, and loosely enough to let the rice expand as it cooks. Each, a uniform cylinder, which she sets in rows in a large pot lined with lamb bones and torn leaves. A second row goes crosswise over the first, and then she places a heavy ceramic plate on top of them to weigh them down. She pours in water to cover the plate, and simmers the pot on the stove.

When she brings them to the table they lie on the plate as symmetrically as they had in the pot. She ladles some broth into a separate bowl, and she sets out a bowl of plain yoghurt, too; it is the traditional way to serve them, though out of all of us, only my father dips the hot grape leaves into the cold yoghurt before he eats them.

"I guess they thought we were strange" is all he has ever said about the way the neighbors looked at *his* mother as she picked the grape leaves along the old mail road. She and my father's father had come from Lebanon, where stuffed grape leaves are an everyday food. But it's not something their neighbors here would have dreamed of making.

I often wonder what those neighbors thought of my grandparents who, having come for work in the mills, had bought a dying farm and settled among them. Maybe because my father has so rarely spoken of it, I imagine suspicion, and wariness. Maybe they waited for failure, though by the time my father was grown, I imagine he looked much like them as he walked through the late fields towards the woods, his rifle slung over his right shoulder, the dusk closing in around him as he called and then listened for his lost hound.

⚘ ⚘ ⚘

I remember when my father drove the tractor as he sprayed the apples, everything but his eyes covered: work gloves, brimmed hat, shirtsleeves rolled down, a bandanna pulled over his nose and mouth. When he sprayed the orchard nearest the house I could hear the halting rhythm of the work — the tractor in low gear, an idle, the spray gun sounding off like pent-up air released. Low gear again, idle . . . Could I smell the spray from my bedroom window? There was something tangy and thick on the air those mornings — he sprayed at dawn, before the breeze came up, so the mist could drift straight down and settle in a fine bloom over the fruit and leaves. The whole orchard shimmered pale and silver-green when he was finished, and my mother spent the next week nagging us to stay out of the apple trees.

One year there was a hailstorm. Hail spat on the roof and rebounded off the granite steps. It sank into the Baldwins, Cortlands, and Northern Spies. The pocks healed, then spread as the apples ripened. Cider, seconds, drops. He kept to the spray schedule anyway, for the health of the wood.

⚹ ⚹ ⚹

Some of the apple boxes come from more than fifty miles away: Upland Farms, Peterborough, New Hampshire is stenciled into the side of several of the boxes, and so is Badger Farms, Wilton, and Moose Hill Orchards, Derry. Apple boxes are often bought second-hand, so the pine is weathered gray, the color of apple bark itself, and no longer smells of resin, but of old soil.

For most of the year the boxes are nested together and stored in a shed — more than a hundred stacks of them, and each stack six or seven feet high. They come into use gradually around mid-August, when the summer apples — Astrakhans, Gravensteins, and early Macs — begin to ripen. We have only a few trees of those varieties and the apples seem incidental among peaches, corn, and tomatoes. Nevertheless it's *their* tight-hearted scent you pick up on a diminishing wind.

September drives down, the Macs are ready to drop, and apple boxes are hauled by the truckload to the orchard. Then the place is littered with pickers — some on the ground, some on ladders, all slung with apple buckets, which are slightly kidney-shaped so they'll fit snugly beneath the chest of a man. The canvas straps are worn low against their shoulders to prevent a sore neck, and I suppose it's those straps that make apple buckets look like collapsed marionettes when they are stowed away at the end of the year, waiting to be taken up by a human hand.

The galvanized buckets have a felt rim to keep the fruit from bruising, and they have a canvas bottom closed by a drawstring so the fruit can be lowered into boxes without being dumped or handled a second time. Eight or nine hours a day, one apple at a time twisted off its stem and placed into the bucket, the bucket filled and loosened into a box — this makes a gentle, clustery rumor — and then again . . .

Macs, Macouns, Cortlands, Baldwins, Northern Spies. So many apple boxes unnested, filled, and stacked beneath the trees — three, sometimes four high. Here and there one of those names reads out from the stacks — Upland, Badger, Moose Hill — orchards now lost to neighborhoods and industrial parks. Or maybe they have simply been abandoned, and the apple trees are rowed among saplings now, their crowns still shaped by the old prunings.

ɬ   ɬ   ɬ

The long hazy days are given over to clear September light. It's on towards evening and I can see Sam's pickup pull into the near orchard. He smokes a leisurely cigarette in the cab of the truck before he steps down and walks toward the Cortland trees. He rubs his grizzled chin. I can hear him whistling. I imagine he's checking to see if those apples are ready to pick. He draws a high branch down and turns over an apple, another, and then releases the branch, which is so heavy it only sluggishly returns to its place. He goes on to another tree. No one could look more assured than he as he sets his gaze ahead and walks further into the orchard.

Why is it so hard for me to see? It's a moment that could keep me here. A moment when I can almost believe those are long strides he is taking straight into the future.

ɬ   ɬ   ɬ

Turn-of-the-century pictures of this farm show a place that is nothing like what I know now. It is almost another country — all pasture and sky, with the house and carriage house and barns in bony relief. Half of those buildings still stand, but the land is long since changed. You'd have to search deep in duff to find traces of the far fields, search beneath needlebed, seedbed, leafbed, because white pines have grown over those fields, pines that are tall and soft and have nothing to do with us. We keep only the near land clear, the choice land, rich and level. And an acre is less work than anything our pre-decessors dared dream. What took them exhausting days to turn over in a cold spring takes part of a morning now. "I can still plow," my father says, "it's no more work than driving a car."

When I was a child there were still a few cleared places that weren't cultivated. The land was marginal or stony and so kept as meadow — a fallow mix of grasses, wildflowers, and weeds — playing field more than anything. They were mowed several times in a summer, not for the hay, but to keep the pines from encroaching. My father was late in years when he began to plant apple trees in those meadows. Cleared places, they seemed, for his dreams and ambitions. He planted redder strains of Cortland and McIntosh, and varieties not found among our old standard trees: Macoun, Jonah Red, Spartan, Empire. Who were they for, those trees? He was late in years, as I say, and hunched down packing in earth around whips that were thin as flyrods.

Anyone who would plant an orchard must be un-daunted by time, willing to wait long years with little chance of seeing the finest seasons. And since an orchard is land narrowed to one crop only, anyone who would plant an orchard must abide by the final decisions. The chosen rootstock, size, variety, the methods of pruning, are promises that can't be gone back on, promises requiring care to the end. So, who were they for? I had nearly forgotten the old faces. I had long swallowed the old names. And now those trees have come to trouble my own future. How much easier for me if those places had remained meadow, playing fields seeded with timothy and redtop. Easier for me if *all* the fields were hay. I can imagine the spare, expansive beauty of timothy and redtop seeded over our whole story, seeded over all the stories, the stones once again unturned, and the soil undisturbed. Nothing there'd be to mark history with, no narrow rings for drought years, no wide rings for plenty, no familiar crowns shaped by hand or shaped by the westerlies. Timothy and redtop give in to all the winds. They'd lie down easily beneath needlebed, seedbed, leafbed, the way this orchard never will. I have dreamt of the long sweep of a burnished inland sea, now glinting and now in shadow, always a bed for my weariness, a resting place for my eyes. I hear the way those grasses make a consoling sound in the wind, a harmony of reeds so unlike the winter branches clattering.

↓   ↓   ↓

People say the Blue Hubbards look like seals resting on the curves of their stomachs. Round-shouldered, full-bellied seals. Blue Hubbards *are* a lumbering kind of winter squash — all middle tapering towards a blunt stem end, and the blossom end can perch like a small, inquiring head. Like seals in shape, yes, but a Hubbard is warty and frosty blue. Its heft is too great and the rind too thick for even a chef's knife to be of much use. You have to drop it on a resistant floor to split it open, or use a cleaver the way my father does when he cuts one up for seed. His aim is as deliberate as a stonecutter's, and the two halves cradle away to reveal a thick wall of orange flesh, its surface mottled with white seeds. He milks the seeds from the flesh and scatters them on newspapers to dry. *Milk* is his word for it, and it does look as if he's working a cow's udder, which he had done as a child and long into adulthood.

There are hybrid vegetables, improved varieties, disease-resistant strains. The kinds of corn my father will grow, or tomatoes, or peppers changes from year to year, and he buys seed from Harris or Agway. Hubbards are one of the last vegetables he still cultivates from its own seed.

Elderly customers are always remembering the nutty, sweet taste of Blue Hubbard and what a smooth pie it makes. But the best Hubbards are upwards of thirty pounds — far too big, they say, now that they live alone. So we split the Hubbards and sell them in quarters or sixths. Some people will still buy whole ones to eat at Thanksgiving or Christmas, kept until then in a dry corner of the cellar — two or three snugged on a shelf as in other years, while outside a shutter whinges, and the blown leaves are covered with frost, then snow.

✶ ✶ ✶

All those people who would rush in at the end of the day to pick up a few things for dinner, they no longer come. There's little left to buy in these last days of October — field pumpkins, Buerre Bosc pears, four kinds of winter squash. The apple crop has dwindled to Baldwin, Northern Spy, and softening McIntosh. Earlier in the year, we harvested the cabbages with their outer leaves intact, and they resembled blown historical roses. Now the exposed parts of the plants are flecked by age and frost, so I strip the outer leaves before putting the cabbage out to sell. Shiny, tight, and pale, those heads seem strangely plain, though no more so than the swept, empty corners of the stand.

We face the same slowdown as always, with drawn-out time between customers who buy a bushel of squash for storage, or a bushel of mixed apples. A woman's brother in New Orleans wants the same Thanksgiving he's always had, and she spends a long while picking out four thick-necked butternuts to ship to him before the holidays. It's not a time to expect anything new. So late last week when I set the walnuts out for sale, every customer had something to say: "For Heaven's sake . . ." "Will you look at that . . ." "Your own walnuts now . . ." "I never knew they'd grow here . . ."

Some would sift through the basket and test the heft of the nuts in their palms. Some would buy a generous pound.

The two walnut trees were a long-ago gift to my father — English walnuts, though a hardy strain from the mountains of Poland. For as long as anyone can remember not one nut had been successfully harvested from those trees. Some years the squirrels got to them; other years the nuts, dry and inedible, rattled in their shells. And no one can say for sure why there was a harvest this year, or if there'll be one again. All we know is that Sallie gathered five bushels from out of the grass and fallen leaves beneath the trees. The leathery husks of the walnuts, split and softened, left a dark stain on her hands as she gathered them and stained her hands again as she scrubbed the husks from the shells: a persistent dye that remained for days in the crevices of her palms.

Five full bushels gathered and scrubbed, then cured in the empty, tepid greenhouse where the men eat their lunch now that it is the warmest spot on the farm. And since there's little left to talk about, they might talk about walnuts while they crack them, as if they were cracking skim ice — with the heel of their palm, or a hammer, or the butt of a trowel. Boat-shaped half-shells litter the greenhouse floor. And the nutmeat, since it is still green, tastes sharp.

Five full bushels is nothing compared to the thousands of bushels of corn, tomatoes, and apples harvested in a year, but walnuts have starred the calendar now, and next year there'll be a handful of customers who say, "Shouldn't the walnuts be ready about now?" Or, "My wife tells me she bought some walnuts here last year." It will be about the time the year tightens. It will be dark before people are halfway home from work — the way it is right now, with the Boston traffic forming a chain of headlights that stretches all the way back to the eastern horizon. The many tired and abstracted, all following the same graceful curve of the road.

⸜ ⸜ ⸜

When I was a child, the Thanksgiving turkeys arrived in late spring. Twelve hundred day-old poults huddled under brooders in the red shed. Some evenings after supper we'd trail after my father as he went to check them. The red shed was stuffy and smelled of hot sawdust; the poults, penned into half of it by high, tightly woven wire. When my father entered the pen, hundreds of poults scattered from where he stepped. He'd grab four, one for each of us. Heads tucked in, they were just palm-sized balls — all heartbeat and nerve. Warm, even to our warm touch. Nervous as they were, a young poult could fall asleep on me in no time. Then its beak might dig hard into my forearm. I remember times I'd jump back it hurt so much, and drop it, and it would tumble into the sawdust and scurry for the brood.

While we held our poults my father saw to the feed and water, and he scooped out the pecked-at chicks and settled them into a small pen of their own. Now and again he'd find a dead one.

It wasn't long before the poults began to grow long in the neck, their heads turned scarlet, their wattles sagged. White feathers sprouted at awkward angles from their backs and wings, and they were herded into the larger open-air coops. The evenings grew longer and we played outside after supper in the willow, or on the rope swing.

All November the phone would ring off the wall with people calling to order their turkeys. My mother would write down their names and the weight they wanted in a large notebook by the phone. Some would request hens or toms. A dozen or so, the largest turkey we had. Extra giblets if we had them. The turkeys would be slaughtered the week before Thanksgiving, and we'd sell them in the five days before the holiday out of what we always called the turkey salesroom.

It doesn't fall in line with the rest of the farm buildings. It's almost domestic: one story of white clapboard with green trim and double-hung windows, six lights over six. There is a small overhang, almost a porch. The door is front and center, and its center panel is glass. I found out a few years back that it had been built as a tea room for my aunt, called "The Red Wing." "You'd be surprised at the business," she told me. "By then there was regular traffic between Lawrence and Lowell. Your grandfather built it for me; brother Charles built the ta-

bles. We sold sandwiches and ice cream, and my pies."
In remembering this she sat on her hands and swung
her legs. She was silent for a moment, and then smiled:
"Anything to keep me home."

In the days before Thanksgiving, my sister, my
brothers, and I would spend much of the weekend and
after-school hours at the salesroom. There was a wood
stove in back, and between customers we'd camp
around it drinking sweet milky coffee. The smell of
wood heat and coffee held sway against the gamy tang
of the fresh killed turkeys just as much as the cold and
the iron light of those short afternoons.

Customers would come and go and we'd try to help,
though most of them insisted on seeing my father.

"Can I help you?" I'd ask.

"Is your father around?"

Those days marked the real end of the farm year, and
everyone, it seemed, would want to close it down with
a little talk. Friends of my father would come in with
gifts — whisky, sometimes Edgeworth tobacco — and
stay awhile. Stories swapped. A pipe lit and then drawn
on. A bottle opened and poured into coffee cups. A final
ease with nothing to do but sell down those turkeys, all
ordered and waiting to be picked up. The last customers would come in at dusk on Wednesday.

My father would always save a few dozen turkeys and
freeze them, which we'd eat on Sundays all through the
next year. And he was always prepared for the inevitable
call on Thanksgiving morning. I think he loved how

the caller would be desperate. They had left their turkey on the porch — there wasn't room in their refrigerator — and the dog had eaten it. They had tried cooking their turkey overnight in a low oven just like the magazine had suggested, and now it was charred beyond recognition. They'd take any size, even a bruised one. Please, did we have any left?

There haven't been turkeys here for twenty years. The new slaughterhouse regulations made it impossible to continue without expanding considerably, and at a considerable cost. In the last years it had been hard anyway for my father to find men willing and able to help with the kill. The turkey coops are storage sheds now. The turkey salesroom — dry and tight — is where Sam stores the seed. Even after all this time my mother gets several phone calls every November — someone inquiring: "You still have the turkeys, don't you?"

↟ ↟ ↟

Only a couple of men stay on to finish out the season, their day beginning in slant light and ending in shadow. There's no hurry now — if it rains or a bitter wind blows in, the work can be put off for a better day since they don't have to keep pace with ripening crops or a parching sun. Water jugs go untouched. It's coffee they drink with their lunch.

They are putting the farm away — cleaning the barn, draining pipes, grading out the last of the stored apples. Machinery is neatly rowed in a shed: tractor, planter, sprayer, harrow, plow. There's frost nearly every morning, and in the orchard all but the last leaves have fallen. You can see how the pruned limbs work out of the squat trunks — the bare wires of a cared-for land.

Now all the fields are in rye. Winter rye is a cover crop only, planted in fields after the corn has been harrowed down. Its dense roots work to keep the long-broken soil from eroding. In mid-September the first planting of it shoots up a minty green, while in other fields squash vines wither to expose tan butternuts, and pumpkins absorb the late sun. By the end of October its deep, even green overlays burnished husks, cobs, and broken stalks. It's a nearly perfect green, without row or furrow, a green that brings up the well-worn roll of the land as it slopes towards the river beyond our view. To those who've worked here all spring and summer and into the fall, the farm now looks surprisingly plain, a landscape only, surveyed and wide under too big a sky. And your eye is drawn to all the slight movements — a hawk, say, and its shadow, or a rabbit scrabbling across matted grass. A deer at the edge of the woods raises its head — such a small stir, no more than an orphaned meteor — and I'm left wondering whether or not I saw it at all.

Wild grasses and orchard grasses turn sere, but winter rye does not. It remains green under accumulating snow, green as ever on south slopes in the January thaws, and everywhere green come the first March floods. Only on the late land — low and boggy, the last to be harvested, and so the last to be put in a cover crop — is the rye grass sparse. There you could count each blade if you wished, and in a dry season unanchored topsoil will blow across the thin snow when gusts come up.

Dusk comes soon enough. The two men hunch in the front seat of their sedan and let the engine warm up a minute before they head home. Lights from their small city star the east hills. One evening planet in the sky before them, the crescent moon growing whiter and harder in the sky behind. Straggling migrations of Canada geese settle in the rye to feed on what remains of the corn. Some evenings they are countless. Even so, they make scarcely a sound. It seems late for them to be this far north, but I suppose it's the plentiful grain that keeps them here, and frozen ground will drive them on.

⌁ ⌁ ⌁

The bright colors are just behind us. No unfallen leaves remain except for clusters of wine-dark ones in the low centers of the oak, and a burnished singular few on the outer branches of the apple trees. It's late. A hunter's shots have scattered through the afternoon.

I am alone on the farmstand when dark comes on, alone as I hasten through the closing chores. I sweep and cash out, then take one last look around before the lights, the lock, the door. I see bare shelves and half-filled bins, a space nearly emptied of its season, its atmosphere filled with the scent of late apples and winter pears — the long slow draft of last things that sweeten only after their harvesting. It marks the end of all we've done, that fragrance, and it dissipates the moment I shut the door behind me, dissipates clear to the first stars of the evening. I sense nothing now but the cold coming on.

It won't be long before those flavors, so keenly deepened, turn at last. The time ahead will in no way resemble the hours already spent. And we, who know only the things of the day, the steady work of our hands, what will we do? It has proved less than a part of all we need, this sift of earth, this deliberate dream.

4

WHITE PINE,
RELICS,
RUST

WHITE PINE is a given name. It has nothing to do with their blue-green needles or their branches, their cones or fissured bark. It isn't tied to their wintry scent. We call them white pines after the quality of their lumber. The dressed wood is the palest of all pines, close-grained, soft, and long-prized.

Always the stories tell how white pines reached over the Northeast — stands of them that neared two hundred feet in height, many so true they were felled for the masts of a foreign navy. The rest: squared off to exhaustion. What remains of those old forests are the stories only, and perhaps a mullion flecked with milk-paint or a floorboard scoured to a deep patina. In early homes I've seen wood panels that must be almost two feet wide, and still I can't comprehend the vanished size of those trees. The white pines I know, the ones I've always believed to be characteristic of these parts, are no more than a century's growth. People call them old field pines because they took hold on abandoned farmland, thriving on thin soil and the bald heat of the days. Their wood is rarely as clear as that of the deliberate primeval growth — boxes, matches, pulp. Still, white pines are the most majestic tree I know.

Behind my house there are four of them that have been full-grown for as long as anyone can remember, and now they must be a hundred feet tall. They're so far above our accustomed sightline of berries, sheds, and fruit trees that my eye is drawn to them from wherever I am on the property. Even when I'm indoors they sometimes come to mind. During a strong night wind I might start thinking they'll go down, though they've withstood a handful of major hurricanes and all the squalls in between. In truth, they are shaped by such exposure: knotted, warty trunks that are too staunch to creak in rough weather, and crowns that lean in from the north as if they've kept the brunt of the wind in them.

In winter gales their boughs don't clatter like the birches. They don't work into your thoughts like the oaks, whose dry leaves rasp. White pine needles are sheathed and soft; their branches, supple as muslin. It's a steady, clear flame of a sound they make. I can hear it way above the roof — ash-throated and abiding.

In the woods where one of the larger trees has fallen, the surrounding ground is flecked with white pine seedlings thriving in that keyhole of light. They are nothing but long soft needles, those young trees, whorls of needles hiding trunks no larger than sticks. Elsewhere, the woods are too dark for the new pines to survive. Instead, hardwoods grow. It seems those other trees will take over later on, but for now white pines are prominent, and after the yellow and red leaves have fallen, those pines stand over the land.

It is then, in winter, that you see how their high-topped crowns are broad and irregular. Some branches shoot away from the rest — out and up — as they follow the lead of the sun. Lower limbs, long blocked from the light, have pruned themselves back to skeletal re-mains — broken, without bark, stained a moss green. The trees don't thicken and crook the way a solitary pine might, but are slender and straight.

I have never seen the owl, though I have heard its call, rounded and hollow. When the winter wind drowns out that call it's the white pines that sound in the woods. With all their length those trunks creak as they sway to the limits of their axis, and the creaking builds and de-cays, builds and decays just as if it were the old uneasy sea pitching beneath them. That creaking dwells in the woods, never clearing the boughs, which have their own sound — a persevering, swept note — distant, with nothing to stop it.

♪   ♪   ♪

I keep my bearings by following the stone walls that fig-ure through these woods. There are breaches in some of the walls where stones have toppled, but many remain as they were built — adroit and lastingly precarious. Every once in a while I come to a place where the walls are seamed clean as fontanels, as if one stone had been fractured somehow. The stones themselves are rarely white or brown — mostly gray, of all shapes, and not often bigger than a man alone could hoist. Exposure has dulled and smoothed their surfaces, in dank places moss grows on them. They are mapped with lichen.

Not long ago these woods were pasture and fields and the walls were made from stones that had been cleared from the land. You'd think there must have been more stone than soil, since I can't begin to count the miles of walls that wind through these woods and the surrounding countryside. And the soil is unpromising still. In our fields, the frost and machinery work new stones to the surface all the time — coarse ones, the quartz still gleaming in them. As ever, they are cleared away. But now they are simply piled in a spare corner of the farm. They're glacial debris, really, rough granites deposited when the last of the ice retreated. The colonists called them fieldstones.

They say it was the European plows that brought so many stones to the surface — the land had never been so thoroughly worked before. And the time told here had never kept so close to the tick of the clock. It couldn't have taken long for the plowed-up stones to dovetail with the need for livestock fencing and a dream of fixed property lines.

Well, property lines vanish as quickly as freak snows, and now these walls seldom coincide with any boundaries on the surveyors' maps. They're relics after the fact, the light we see from collapsed stars. Some edge roads and fields as if still in place, but largely it's through these woods they maze — gapped and turned back on themselves like an old woman's furred-in thoughts.

    ↙ ↙ ↙

It's after snowmelt and the early rains, and the brook has settled back into its old known bed. Just last week the flood current poured over the smaller sounds, but now that the flow has calmed, each disturbance — eddies, channels, near water falling over roots and tumbled granite — makes its own soft-throated sound, and I can't hear the end of them as I sit by this broad place in the stream where moss-covered stones scatter through the bed. A child could cross stone to stone, and here is where we did cross as children, tottering over the water, our arms outstretched for balance.

If I just sit in this one place and gaze at the sunlit water, and listen, and breathe in the spring green, I can almost believe it's as cool and removed as when I would come here thirty years ago, here just to be away. A child picking her way through the tangled fallen brown of these April woods. It smells faintly of skunk cabbage, whose purple hoods mottle the low places. The fiddle-heads are curled tight in their papery cauls. The shaded remove of an already removed place.

Our farm lies at the eastern edge of what is now a moderate, sprawling town. Though this had long been an agricultural community, by the time I was school-aged it was edging towards suburbia, and there weren't many farmers' children left. School was on the other side of town, in the most built-up and densely populated area — a far journey there, and an even farther journey home — a crossing, really, back into my own world. The area around the school was a city to me. The cotton mill at the Beaver Brook dam and the blonde brick Catholic church rose above squat businesses. There was almost no breathing room between Turner's hardware — sacks of Blue Seal out front, pickup trucks pulled up alongside — and Brown's Appliances, where the white enamel stoves gleamed in a sturdy row behind the plate glass. Village Pizza, Dalton's Ice Cream, Rosie's Variety, which except for the Squirt and Marlboro signs seemed a shingled cottage among the storefronts. There were pots of geraniums on the stoop in spring. Becket's Cleaners, LeBlanc's Real Estate, Marie's Doughnuts — at that hour, a stretch of mostly empty stools, maybe an old man rereading his newspaper, a younger one bent to the contents of his briefcase, two women talking and sipping coffee.

After a few miles the businesses fell away, and our foreheads rested against the glass. The driver downshifted as we turned from the state road onto Coburn Road, the first of a network of back ways that made up the rest of the route home. They were the old two-rod roads, my father has told me, originally measuring two rods wide from stone wall to stone wall. They used to be the one way from farm to farm, from farm to town. At a few points along the route I could see them pay out across the territory for miles ahead, breaching the hills and scribing the broad valleys, but mostly the roads were so curved they only opened up right in front of us, suddenly revealing the old houses built into the bend in the road or at a convergence of slopes. They sit at the heart of their land, those houses — worlds of their own — surrounded by barns and outbuildings, maybe a windmill, a silo. Pollen clots the hand-dug pond. And their fields stretch away in every direction.

By the time our bus traveled those roads, many of the farmers, even if they kept a small dairy herd, had other jobs, too. The acreage had closed in on their home- steads, and the spaces between sprouted clusters of sub- divisions, little mazes that stopped abruptly as they had begun, like those towns floating on the Kansas plains. The streets that reached back — horseshoes, or grids, or circles — weren't guided by fences, and had no des- tination other than to return to the old road. I could see down whole rows of houses waiting to settle. Clapboard capes, half-bricked garrisons, low ranches — more sim- ilar than the lives inside could possibly have been — were built where they had been marked no matter the lay of the land. They set squarely in the center of their lots, parallel to the road. And a planted tree — split leaf or red leaf maple — in every yard, equidistant between the house and the road. Basketball hoops on the garage peaks. Hopscotch squares chalked on the drives. The bus would slow at the first corner of the development, and all at once six, eight, ten children would gather their books, file out the open door, and scatter like struck marbles.

The busload lightened to a handful of children and the houses drew farther and farther apart. My cousins, my sister, my brothers, and I were the last stop in the afternoon. Winters we'd step down into the approaching dusk. In the east a lone radio tower pulsed red just above the oaks. The evening paper had already come, and I'd collect it at the mailbox and go in.

The distance that bus traveled is almost nothing to me now, but it's also true, of course, that the world has closed in. To be a child here would hardly be the same. Even the far edges of these woods have been claimed by houses. I now see lights through the trees to the north where once the view had nothing human in it. The new people are more affluent than those who had come here when I was a child, and their houses are larger and more elaborate. The lots, larger; the landscaping, more elegant.

Yet among these subdivisions, there are still a good handful of dairies, orchards, produce farms, about the same size as ours. Every once in awhile another may fold — the taxes are high, and the land values are high, as are start-up costs, so if there's no one in the family to take on the work, it's unlikely the farm can continue. There are flare-ups with each new development. Old residents can be cold-eyed about the new ones; new residents are never prepared for, say, the smell of Thayer's pigs or his piles of spare parts and tractor tires, the rusted rainwater pooling in his yard, the plastic on his windows all summer long.

Many of those families in the houses between farms are faithful to the locally grown corn and tomatoes, and they carry home their milk in glass bottles. They may stop by the stand three or four times a week. "I wish you were open year round," one says to me. Another, "I tell my daughter this is our garden." And, another, spending a good while longer than really necessary choosing her apples, tells me it's nice we're here as I ring up her order. Then, "Don't ever sell."

It's not a sentiment I've ever heard expressed by those who live farther away. Many of the customers who come from Lowell or Lawrence speak Spanish or Khmer, and when they come to weigh and pay for their produce, their children, some of them no older than seven or eight, speak to me in English, "How much for this?" then turn to their parents and speak in their own language. And turn to me again with payment. If there are no children, we might negotiate wordlessly. A man holds up three cucumbers with one hand and I pick the correct change out of the coins he holds in his other, open palm. "Thanks." He nods or closes his eyes and then opens them again, and heads away.

As the last of the open land, this part of town is zoned for industry. A dreamscape for everyone who runs for selectman, since they can conjure jobs and an expanded tax base out of the deep woods. And there has been some development. What was once the old Coburn land quickly became a regional office of New England Telephone. As fluorescent surveyors' flags appeared, the talk geared up. I'd hear it at the stand. A man working his toothpick against an incisor saying: "I hear two hundred trucks a day will be heading towards the interstate."

And the man answering him shaking his head: "They say they'll be starting at 6:00 A.M."

"That early, really?"

"Don't think the road can handle it."

"I know, I know."

It's only been a few years since the phone company went in, but already it's hard for me to remember what the woods there looked like. We get a flurry of the linemen's trucks pulling in the stand at the end of the day. There's one who loves spinach — he keeps telling me to sauté it with garlic and olive oil. Another buys a Bosc pear and a McIntosh for his next day's lunch.

It's built up enough here now so that if you have a far point in mind you might pass by without noticing the butternuts full in the September sun, or — if it's mid-July — that the Seneca Brave is ripe and the talk of all our talk. There have been customers — strangers — surprised to find us here. I remember one woman who wouldn't believe our cleared land could produce enough to fill up the stand. She asked me, "Where's the farm?"

"Here."

"Where?"

"Here," I said again and swept my hands full circle.

"For all this? I don't believe it. They must buy some of this stuff. Are you sure they don't buy some of this?"

"*We* grow it here."

The rare times larger animals cross through anymore — they are being squeezed out to the north — they cause enough mayhem for a story in the local paper. It was front-page news when a black bear cub came out of these woods and squalled across the fairway of the nearby golf course. Sometimes the stories even make the Boston paper, as when late last summer a bull moose broke out of the pines and trampled across the back yards on Cedar Lane. By the time the first squad car appeared it had made its way to Hawthorn Road, where the officers called for backup. "It's the size of a horse" came the plea over the scanner, which brought countless curiosity seekers along with three more patrol cars. In the end they were as helpless as the first, except for keeping the people at a safe remove as they waited for the expert marksman, who was to shoot the moose full of tranquilizers. It took a while for the drug to take effect, and that huge mammal splashed through a built-in swimming pool — as he emerged the water sheeting off him sounded like a waterfall — and knocked over a gas grill before he turned, bewildered, towards the crescent of onlookers, and crumpled against a lawn chair.

Even so, some still come here, as I think the bagpiper must, because it does seem remote. I have heard him playing his pipes at the cemetery. Sometimes he's in full dress as he stands at the top of the hill. He has his back to the woods and faces out across the graves towards our fields as he plays. I don't recognize the tune — it seems a long sequence of variations. His drone pipes carry farthest on the cloudy days, a mournful bray, the music itself making the place feel lone and distant.

And by this brook, on a mild spring afternoon, there's enough woods left for much to remain hidden. I rarely see the deer, but I do see their sign — scat, ragged browse, and the path they've worn along the water's course. Sometimes I hear coyotes from my bed as I try to sleep. Their calls harp on the storyless night and, same as strangers, they set all the dogs barking.

♪ ♪ ♪

This land has a kind old roll to it. Subdued hills stretch on for as far as I can see, their slopes as gradual as the hips and shoulders of a figure in repose. Or I'm reminded of the fluid curve of starlings sweeping towards a lone tree. Nothing remains — not that the scanning eye can see — of the obtrusive, jagged peaks of earlier ages. Nothing of a time when lichen and moss were the only green; and sound, a stone tumbling down the scree. Erosion and long, slow accretions turned those ages into quiet country; and that country has been worn to these broad valleys and low rises by quickening

streams veining the soil on their way to the sea. Geol-
ogists say these hills are what remains of a peneplain,
which means *almost a plain*, and if you search back far
enough you can find *patience* in the word.

The Pennacooks farmed it first, without a wheel or a
plow, in fields they'd cleared with granite axes and fire.
They didn't turn over the earth, but used spades made
from the shoulderbones of deer, or kept to the lighter
soils where a planting stick could make a hole for seed.
Everything hoed and hilled and harvested by hand.
They say you could smell the herring buried in the
older lands, and that the fields looked nothing like the
ordered rows I know — one crop planted alongside another so that the hard northern flint tasseled above
beanstalks or a tangle of pumpkin vines. I imagine it was
hard to tell where their care left off and the wilderness
began. At the edge of their fields they thinned the
grapes and wild berries. In the forests beyond, to im-
prove the hunting, they set fires to keep down the saplings and brambles. Footfalls on duff sounded softer
than the beat of a siskin's wing. In the long winters, cut
pumpkins, dried beans, and braided seedcorn lay deep
in their stores. Now a white stone washes onto my path,
and I can't tell for sure if it's rough quartz or quartz
worked into a spearpoint or knife.

The English settlers cleared those fields more thoroughly, and cleared their hunting grounds and fishing
camps and settlements until the land resembled a
woven pattern of holdings: small blocked-out acres of

tillage and pasture divided by fences and hedges or a thin line of trees that bordered a stream. As before, corn, squash, and beans. Also cattle, poultry, and sheep. And teamed oxen — heads down, wide-eyed, straining against a yoke. You could hear their labored breath as they worked across the heavier soils. You could hear struck metal — curt, then reverberant — belling across the open fields as shoes and blades were hammered into shape.

One of the old plows hangs in the back of the barn. The handle is fashioned from clear-grained wood, and it has an iron coulter. I can see how the man behind guided his own dreaming, which yielded only to the contours of these hills. Dreams laid down on soil full of stones and early frost. Soil thinning down the hundreds of years of such dreams — children and children's children in a cloud of raised dust behind the oxen, or raising their scythes to mow a field, stepping into the stubble they themselves had made to sweep the blade again and further the swath in the grasses. The hay wilted, then dried, and as it dried its scent lingered to the day that one mower hung up his blade on the low branch of an oak tree and walked off to join the Union cause.

That story about the scythe is a story from states away, but it could have happened here, too. My father told us about it once when he came back from the woods after finding a horseshoe embedded in the trunk of a maple. He supposed someone had hung the shoe on the tree maybe fifty years ago and, as the tree grew, it grew around the shoe. "Just like that scythe in the oak," he said, to which the mower never returned. To this day it hangs on the branch, its grip worn by weather, the blade's arc gone into the growth rings.

I've seen the lists of the Civil War dead from the small towns near here. The same few surnames — Richardson, Varnum, Coburn, Clough — scroll down the page. And those who returned had seen firsthand the long growing seasons to the south and the richer topsoil to the west, against which their own toughed-out acres must have seemed like folly. Why wouldn't they dream of the tall grass prairies, and of being the first to turn over such soil — stone-free, level, and deep in loam? I was thirty before I'd ever driven west, and I couldn't stop looking at the long horizon. The plantings disappeared straight into it, and there was always that sky. I remember the small towns floated like islands among the crops, and every made thing seemed outsized — the barns, the silos, those combines. When we say *farm*, I said to myself, we don't mean the same thing.

The war only hastened the long slow abandonment of the New England land, which the opening up of the West had made inevitable. There was no way to compete with crops being grown more cheaply and efficiently on better soils, or soils that simply had not yet been exhausted. The poorer upland farms were the first to go, though I still see one now and again — a handful of cattle wandering a rocky slope or picking out grasses among the pines, a wrackline of saved, rusted machinery alongside the house. One light selves the night, and every time I pass by I wonder *who* or *how*?

With their alluvial soils, the better valley farms hung on, but you could no longer shout the news from farm to farm. In some places, white pines reclaimed the abandoned land between them, and elsewhere mill cities — seemingly sprung whole from the heads of new dreamers — were built along the river. Within a dozen years the Merrimack had been dammed in a handful of places, and red brick factories lined stretches of its banks. In every city, high as the church spires, came a clock — four faces to the cardinal points so you could read the hands from any place in the city. The daughters of the farmers read them from their dormitories, which were often built of the same brick as the factories. On their way to work their footfalls drowned in the countless echoes of others, and once there, the air was white with clothdust.

The pace of building outpaced the ability of farm families to supply the mills with labor, and eventually the work force had to be drawn from other countries. Both my parents' families came here at the end of the last century to work in those mills, and sometimes I'm not sure which side of the family the stories come from — stories about strict time, the boss over them, Bread and Roses. How all the doors in the tenements opened at the same time every morning as the city set off for work. My mother's family stayed in Lawrence, and her father worked as a weaver all his life. My father's family bought this farm a dozen years after they came here.

"Jesus, I don't know how they got the money together," my father says, and I think he still remembers every trip to the bank and how much the corn on the School Road sold for in 1931. In his story about the red heifer, who had six or seven lactations and was still called the red heifer, he remembers how much she yielded and the exact price of her milk for years on end.

Most of the farms that survived survived on their dairy herds. Their connected buildings, which made for easy passage in winter, have created the classic picture we hold in our heads: a beauty of form and line, angled and neat against the lush summer hills. A moderate slope to the roofs; the doorways, plainly framed. Children made a song of those structures as they played their games in the south-facing yards, chanting *big house, little house, backhouse, barn.* Front parlors, summer kitchens, the scent of lilac. Their marker trees shade our driveways, and the peonies they planted to make a tea for nightmares are arranged in vases on our tables.

I like to imagine the journey of that milk, how it was a scant seven miles from here to where it was finally set on a doorstoop in Lawrence. It began in the calm of predawn, and the cattle shifting in their stalls. The air in the barn is warm with the heat of the animals, and humid. It smells of hay and dung. The tin swallows its own resonance as the milk fills the pails. "I can't believe they trusted me with the milk," my aunt keeps saying these days. "I wasn't more than five or six — tiny — and they had me carry it all the way to the well." It would stay cool there until the wagon from the creamery came to collect it. As the wagon worked back out of the yard, the burdened wheels turned slowly. The sky just beginning to pale. In the east, the last slip of the moon.

At the creamery the milk was combined with the milk from other farms, poured into clear glass quarts, and loaded into another wagon to be distributed to the households in the city. The glass sweats. The road is cobblestone now, and the bottles chime softly as they nudge against one another. A child jostles among them. In his backward view, the buildings lining both sides of the streets rush away. The shod hooves clatter and set off sparks as they strike the cobbles. When the road crosses the Merrimack at the Great Stone Dam the water pouring over the boards is loud enough to take away his thoughts, and he can hear that roar until the wagon turns away from the river and into the maze of lanes and alleys where people live.

As he climbs the stairs to set the milk on the landings of the tenements, his boots scuff the sunk well in the middle of each step. The paint, if there had been paint at all, is worn to bare wood from all the comings and goings. Sometimes he hears a scurrying before his steps. He sees shadows — or is it a man? — moving among wooden barrels. So early, and already so much going on. Many voices through the doors — the murmuring of those who've just woken, and must get on with the day. And children calling names he's never heard — *tante* . . . He smells yeast proofing, and bread baking, and long-lingering spices. Alcohol. Urine. Naphtha and lanolin come in on a small wind. He is supposed to be quick at this — three landings in each tenement, and he has to leave the milk at the foot of each entrance and pick up the empty bottles left for him. As he runs back down the stairwells — the man at the reins is impatient — the empty glass against empty glass sounds just like ice falling from the pine branches in the January thaw.

The way the ice is falling now in the woods behind my house, from pines that have grown up just since the hurricane, on the same land that may have been Pennacook hunting lands, and then the cleared fields of an early settler. Even so, the lay of the land itself — those payed-out hills — is still so much the same. And the changes wrought — the ways of understanding, of forging tools, of telling time, the negotiated shapes we dream — what do they mean against such patience? That dairy herd is gone as well. There is a dump in one of the low places in the woods where my father has abandoned the things from those years. Milk cans, like nurse logs, are half sunk in the soil. Their exposed parts are already thinned to tracery. Some bottles are there, too, and on days like this — warm after a winter storm — I can't tell what is shattered and glinting — the fallen ice, or glass.

♪   ♪   ♪

When the barn was thick with animal warmth, snow melted as it fell on the roof. Now that nothing but tools and machinery are stored here, the barn is cold in winter. On windless days it is almost as cold as the open air, and snow accumulates on the roof, in some years lingering into March.

One day voices echo in the frost, the next they are lost in the sound of the thaw. This morning water blistered along the edge of the barn roof and began to drip — in measured time at first — and then it quickened as the day grew warmer. By noon it seemed that all the snow of the lean months was streaming off the roof. The dripping incised channels in the accumulated snow around the barn, and then worked channels into the ground itself — lines more true than those of the building, which has long since sighed and settled.

Lines as true as the ones in the carpenter's dream. One man built every barn still standing along this road. No one remembers his name, but you can tell his work by certain details. Above the door he always hung a row of six lights, which sometimes fogged with the pluming breath of the herds.

*   *   *

The milk room was always slab-cool and dank. A square fieldstone room in the southeast corner of the barn, it has one window — four lights painted shut. Years ago they stored the fresh milk there, but the last of the dairy herd was sold way before I was born. Pasture turned to cropland, and we store baskets of harvested crops in the milk room: beans, cukes, tomatoes, summer squash, green peppers.

Where some of the pasture has grown into woods, the stone walls are strung with rusted barbed wire, and every once in a while you'll see a tree growing up through the wire. There'll be a broad welt on the bark where the strands have healed into it. The disused mail road runs along some of the walls. Tangled slash and undergrowth have not yet encroached on it, and the wheel ruts are apparent. My brothers, sister, and I wore the right one to a narrow track of dirt the width of a foot. The left one is faint and grassy.

⚹ ⚹ ⚹

Heaped in the corners of the barns and shed, or slung on driven nails there, are the scythes and harnesses, the horse-driven harrows and plows. A sower's apron, a grain scoop, a hayrake put away for the day that turned into years, then into seasonless decades. Crusted, creaky things, with gray dust sifting off them. Beyond the reach of the sun and the damp night air, unstirred by passing voices or the swallows nesting in the beams, they await the last say, like dear letters before the final parting — packeted, stored, and — since every end can still be believed — sometimes unfolded and read for remembrance.

When I poke around in those corners, I almost always find things I want to take home where I can scrub the must from them, and make the grain come up, or a blade brighten, or the cracked leather soften. Old tools become my doorstops and bookends and range on the kitchen sill. I've hung the drafthorse's hammered shoe above my doorway, and packed soil into milkpails to set pansies in.

Many are the things I find that I can't identify; when I show them to my father his memory jars, and he'll ask, "Where did you find that?" or exclaim, "Why, that's an antique . . ." then tell me it was what they'd used to saw the pond ice, or cut the curd, or funnel sap. The day I showed him the fawn-footed handle of an ax, he turned it over, and tested the feel of it in his hands. He must have remembered his old strength as he tightened his grip. I swear his look was to warn me again that any tool will falter in an unskilled hand.

✦ ✦ ✦

People mark time by the '38 hurricane. "That stand of pines has been there since before the hurricane," they say, or, "The stream didn't pass that way until after the hurricane." Big stories about the storm come from the coast: buses swept off roads, the late summer gentry caught watching from their windows — the way they always watched line storms — as seas broke over their houses.

We're thirty miles inland, and a good distance from the Merrimack, so the stories we hear aren't about floods and tides. Our place was all wind, sounded by things in its way — branches, clapboards, loose panes. Wind flattened the cowshed, they say, and pried the well cover from the well. It knocked over fences, both whitewashed and stone, and sheared laden branches off the apple trees. In the cemetery it uprooted a grave. Wind turned the woods into a foreign place — a haphazard horizon full of slash and sky; trees strewn every which way, exposed sapwood, and gapes to draw a stare, I imagine, like powerlines cut through the wilderness or ski trails on a summer mountain.

All my uncles love to tell how they worked long days hauling hurricane lumber to the mill. It took them years just to clean up their own little woodlot, they say. I've seen pictures of them, leaning on axes, hats jaunted back on their heads. They're posing by downed trees, and seem like victors in the photographer's eye.

⚡ ⚡ ⚡

Monadnock. The exact meaning of the Algonquin word is lost. Some people believe *manitou* — a guardian spirit — is stowed in the name. Others safely say that it means "mountain that stands alone." Monadnock rises only a few thousand feet above its surrounding countryside, but it *is* solitary, with long gradual slopes, and so seems imposing. And it is all the more imposing because its summit is bare rock, so that when the lower land is running with the thaw, bringing out new scents and bringing up the color of lichens, the snowed-in peak of Monadnock keeps its cold look.

Between the ice age and the present day there was a time when the summit of that mountain was covered in red spruce — a pure stand, dark green and resinous. Those trees must have played down the elements, or they took on the brunt of them. Anyway, they protected the soil, and the summit's amber duff — color of steeped tea — just kept getting deeper and softer.

The stories I've heard say the fires began soon after the region was settled. Fires to clear pasture. Fires that had spread too far up the mountain and burned until they burned themselves out. The one fire that was so hot it killed the red spruce and the soil they grew on. The charred trunks fell where they stood — a black tangle that became a haunt for wolves. It was early in the nineteenth century when the dead timber was deliberately set ablaze to drive the wolves from that place. What remained — ash and barren soil — easily blew away on the constant wind. So, the summit will always be bare, they say, since the weather is just too persistent for the new soil to establish itself, and the old berry-pickers' paths are just too well traveled.

At the summit, cold-chiseled into the rock, I find initials and dates that go back into the last century. As the surrounding land has become more widely settled, the climb has become more popular, since it isn't difficult, and from the top you can see far in every direction. To the northwest rises Mt. Mansfield in Vermont; east of north, Mt. Washington; north of east, in Maine, Mt. Agamenticus. To the south is a quieter breath, the low-lying hills of eastern Massachusetts. Those hills have no focus — except for the higher towers of Boston — since they're nearly even in height.

When I look out from the top of Monadnock I know the farm is off to the east and south, but I can't pick out where it must be. All contour is gone — the hills we plow and build into, the low place in the orchard where the frost lingers, the rise where, early on, the lights of a small city might climb towards Orion. It appears as if all the land has healed back into a plain, the working of all that water seeming to have disappeared, and along with it the barns and fields have disappeared, the back stoops, the millstack, the stone church. Detail lost to the color of a cold flame, as lost as the towns beneath the Quabbin Reservoir, which supplies much of that southern stretch of land with water.

The old residents of those drowned towns hold re-unions now and again to recall the scent of the honey-suckle or the sweet taste of a sheepnosed apple — the last details, the way my aunt will recall, not the herd, but her cheek resting against the pied flank of the cow as she finished the milking.

*   *   *

One of our fields runs right up to the west wall of the Richardson Cemetery, and springtime burials can put a stop to work there. The sound of the harrow — like a jangling chain — and the entrenched engine noise of the tractor drown out voices, so Sam will stop the machinery as the funeral procession makes its turn into Richardson gate, and he'll wait out the burial service. The worked-over soil is to his left; unbroken land, to his right.

It's not the oldest of cemeteries, and many of the gravestones are from recent years: large, polished granites, headstones on shoulders of stone. On that small wooded hill they appear almost too large, the same as deep sea vessels anchored in a snug harbor.

Almost always you can see surviving family members attending those graves. By the first of December, balsam wreaths are strapped to the granite markers, and potted poinsettias — silk or plastic — are set atop the small garden beds in front of the stones. Every year one woman hangs miniature ornaments from the shrubs that flank her husband's grave. Nearly every grave is decorated for the Christmas season, and also for Easter, when cream-colored lilies plume against the polished side of the stones. At other times of the year the decorations are not as widespread, but they are consistent. On Mother's Day the cemetery will have its own pattern of floral arrangements, different from that of Father's Day. Every veteran's grave is flagged at the end of May, and when Halloween comes, pumpkins of all sizes are placed alongside the graves of those who died young. In the course of the year such configurations are nearly as predictable as the appointed turns of the constellations — when Orion rises in the east at sundown, when the Dipper begins it decline, when the Pleiades, the deep-seated Pleiades, is overhead at midnight.

To the north of Richardson Cemetery is a smaller, older graveyard — Bailey Cemetery. Its markers hold the names of the settlers — Coburn, Austin, Clough — and are mostly portal shaped, some of black slate, stained with lichen. They are half-sunk and skewed. At times passersby will stop to make parchment rubbings of their carved details. Or they'll puzzle over the epigraphs, and finally smile: *Beloved of Almon. She hath done what she could. I shall return to her, but she shall not return to me.*

No one remembers the last burial there, and I have never seen flowers set against the stones, though towards the end of May, veterans will see that the soldiers' places are marked just as they are in every other cemetery in town, and early on Memorial Day those veterans pay their tribute: seven guns fired three times, then a patient and clear trumpet. It is just after dawn. The road is still. The ceremony is witnessed by no one now that all the nearby children are grown. There must have been a dozen years when we'd crouch beside the cemetery wall to wait out the long, single line of taps so we could search the grass for shell casings before being called back to the house for breakfast.

⚘ ⚘ ⚘

The worked-out tractor stops an access road. The lame harrow has been pulled to the inside corner of a fence. And the old planter — at station among shattered grasses by the barn. It's likely they have been rusting for longer than they labored, having been hauled to marginal places after they broke a final disk, say, or were shadowed over by new machinery. After a good rain, the low ground around them puddles with copper-colored water. Rusted to fine things, they are, nearer to script or to vertebrae than the forged shafts, axles, and tines. Who, anymore, can imagine they were once bent to a human will — these that thin and crumble to so much ferrous duff?

And who isn't inclined to think of them as being closer to draft horses at pasture than to the machinery we now use? A new Case tractor parades across the years we have, hauling beamy harrows, planters, and cultivators. A giant bucket attaches to the front of the tractor and is used to move loam or to clear a way for drainage. We tell our time by those outsized wheels that make their slow, peremptory turns and lay down chevron tracks on the soil.

And yet, in the wake of that tractor, not much is changed from other years. Disks and tines disturb the earth at standard intervals. Hybrid seed funnels through the planter and drops out in traditional increments — so many inches between stalks of corn, so many between beans, between cabbage plants . . . East, west, and east again, measured lines follow the well-worn roll of the land.

Scours on stone made by glaciers, scours made by harrows. Where is the trained eye to distinguish one from the other? The distance between the past and ourselves is as thin as the saturated red enamel on the new tractor, though we can't bring ourselves to believe its durable surface will rust. And besides, the machines are too big to be simply left to one side. Imagine this tractor in disuse, and how it would block the easy line of the horizon. Sharp edges in a hazy season. Orchard grasses would never clear the hubs of the wheels, and the raised bucket stalled above the cab would remind us of a saurian jaw and the creatures of a vanished epoch.

5
WINTER

In the mudroom, Hubbard seeds are scattered on newspapers to dry. Winter rye has come up in the cornfields. Apple branches are sprung and still except for a topmost bough here and there, still laden, that had been impossible to reach no matter how the ladder had been angled. The stand, swept clean and shut up.

No one ever buys more than one red cabbage – one lasts weeks. Six rows weren't picked clean before the hard frost and haven't been plowed under. The frozen heads appear from a distance: perfect, the color darkened to burgundy. This morning's windless snow is melting back, exposing the red cabbage, all that's visible.

Even under a changeless sky my father tunes in the weather half a dozen times a day. The strong, unhurried voice of the forecaster seems to carry an honest weight across a great distance, since every sentence rises from and decays back into a sieve of static. He knows the litany by heart — daily extremes in temperature, the barometric reading, the extended forecast. Then the voice runs on through peripheral facts — the winds atop Mount Washington, temperatures in Hartford and Providence, Marblehead tides, Boston tides, Hyannis . . . A few are places he has never been.

Now the voice says rain will continue on into the afternoon. If this rain had fallen a few weeks back, he would have worked through the morning anyway, dressed in his yellow oilers that stand out against the drenched land like a blaze on bark. But it is November. There are no crops and little work, and the rain falls without consequence. Even so, by force of habit, he sizes it up. This was the best kind — teeming, soaking deep into the ground. It could rain a long time like this and not cause runoff or flash flooding. The damp air has seeped into the house and so, for the first time this year, he turns on the heat, and he can smell dust burning off the pipes and radiators. Though it is still midmorning he switches on the light above the sink. Water dripping and a fine water falling are the only sounds from outside, since the rain has quieted the mockingbird, which was nearly quiet, anyway, so late in the year.

♪ ♪ ♪

"Is that you?" I asked as I pulled the old photo from a box of photos. It was a summer day in the picture, and the child who stared straight ahead was no more than four, chubby and dark haired, in an oversized dress and scuffed boots. She was alone and holding on to a fence. "Oh!" my mother said as she took the photo from me. That was all.

The stories my mother tells of her childhood are spare. I know her parents came here before they were twenty from a village in Campania. I know they sailed from Naples and continued to speak Italian for the rest of their lives, though my mother would answer in English. My grandfather insisted on it, the way he insisted on living on the third floor of the tenement for the light and air. "Those stairs kept me slim," my mother now says.

The photographs from her life before marriage are also spare. The one I pulled from the box is the only one I've ever seen of her as a child, though there are a few formal portraits of her in her twenties. The others were lost, she guessed, in the time after her father's death when they broke up her parents' apartment. Their keepsakes had been stored in the top drawer of the dresser, which they had sold along with the rest of the furniture. And that apartment — it was razed thirty years ago, though I can still recall it. Well, a few shards of it. I remember a low coal fire and a bed by the stove. And the way my grandmother gestured good-by — with her palm facing away from me, and opening and closing her hand, so that I thought she was beckoning me back.

To me, my mother's past is made up of such discrete

moments, almost as neat as the attic she keeps, which she is always cleaning. If she adds to its store, she is sure to take away by sending my father's old clothes or our old toys to the Goodwill. Of course, there are things that will always remain, though they may never be used again — a silver service, the wedding dress, a box of baby slippers and bracelets, the pictures of us children.

She was always carrying a camera as we were growing up. In some of the shots we're in the same poses year in and year out: the four of us in descending order in front of the fireplace or crowded on the stairwell on Christmas morning. Each of us stands alone and in white under the variegated maple on the morning of our First Holy Communion. I've found a whole box of photos of my sister in her ballet outfit. She is standing center stage in no recognizable pose. Or she is tiptoeing in a circle with other children. Although I know she threw a tantrum before every class, there are enough photos so you'd think that dance became her life.

My mother is always remembering us in fine detail, even now as she is growing forgetful about her daily life and has to write everything down: a list by the telephone — *dentist, sisters, milk*; a scrap of paper marked *gas* stuck through the keychain; and days on the calendar written over with *Maggie, trash, lunch*. It's not unusual for her to forget what we talked about yesterday. Or if she remembers, she is no longer sure she remembers correctly: "We're going to Lawrence . . . at three . . . tomorrow. Right?"

Sometimes we joke about it, sometimes I grow impatient. A little afraid. How can this be when she even remembers my father's past clearly? She has heard his stories so many times that they have begun to lap over her own early years. She might just as well have been there, too, to see his uncle waste away with a blood disease, though he died before she even knew my father. She nods as my father tells how he came out to the farm to spend his last days in the summer air and all you could see of him was his wool blankets as he sat out back huddled against the Baldwin tree.

♪　♪　♪

On warmer days my father speeds the pickup across the hardened field to the last standing rows of cole crops. The cabbage is punky and smells high, but there might be a small cauliflower bound tight in its leaves and only touched by frost. My mother thaws the cauliflower by soaking it in a bowl of water until it comes up to temperature, then she pares away the damaged parts. It is not a necessity, this. He just likes to rummage around in the ragged end of the season and salvage what he can. She goes along with it — or waits it out — until the deep snow.

She has lived more than half her life in this sprawling, sturdy house among fields to which she brought little more than her parents' picnic basket woven of ash. I have heard most of the stories about the city of Lawrence from my father who never lived there. He is the one who tells us again that the main street was cobblestone, just like Paris or Rome, and the shod horses sent sparks flying. He tells how the Italians buried their fig trees to protect them from frost, and he describes the trench they'd dig alongside the trees and how they'd bind the crowns and cut away the far roots before tipping them into the ground, just the way her father did in his garden in that city where the snow slushed under hooves and boots, and turned brown as the canals.

Here snow weighs on the bull pine and the turned branches of the pear, it settles on the lead-white sills and in the empty open greenhouse. It ghosts the sere vestige of a garden. The darkened outshot of the house is closed off, and snow accumulates in perfect arcs against the frosted windows of those rooms. In the lit rooms where my parents live snow flecks the panes — a sound softer than the click of needles shaping a sleeve of nubbed wool, sound of a mouse too small to leave tracks on solid ground.

⚘ ⚘ ⚘

The two muddy wheel ruts have been paved into even, cambered hardtop. There's traffic at all hours, especially around dinnertime. From the farmhouse kitchen my aunt sees headlights going west and taillights going east, more lights than stars, more outside than in. She shuts one lamp off behind her and turns one lamp on ahead of her as she moves along the downstairs rooms. A house lived down to a single light isn't something she ever would have imagined. For so many years there were two shifts at the table for dinner, and she couldn't get a word in edgewise. Tuesdays she'd bake at least eleven pies, and Wednesdays the bread.

What has remained the same? The carriage house has always been white, and the weathervane always a mare. The house itself has been painted brown, and then painted gray; the upstairs fireplaces sealed, the silo blown down in a hurricane. One brother after another married, except for Cal who always had to have two eggs over easy for breakfast and a hot meal for lunch and dinner.

There were the three of them for the longest time — she and her sister Alice, and Cal. She did all the cooking except at holidays, when Alice would take all that time making the cookies, hundreds of them shaped the same. Cal has been dead these three years, and Alice three more. Their clothes hang in the closets. Visitors have slept in their beds. My father left that house well over forty years ago, when there were still seven at home, and now he stops in every day to make sure she has taken her pills. He knocks, and enters before she can answer. The rooms are quiet enough to stun anyone at first, and he starts with the smallest talk: "How cold did it get here last night?" "Has anyone called?" "Are your groceries holding out?" He goes over her mail and sets aside the bills to be paid. If it's winter he might suggest she visit the brothers in Florida. "There's nothing to worry about. I'll put you on the plane at Logan and Charlie will meet you at the airport in Tampa." She never agrees. He checks her pill box and the expiration date on her milk.

There are sparks you can blow on for a little heat. Sometimes old lost things take flame. Today he has stayed on longer than usual, and they are talking of the time before the silo blew down in the hurricane. The streetlights have flickered on, and the traffic's picked up going west.

↗   ↗   ↗

Shadows sharp as substance. The long road white with salt. Through the bare branches I can see every buried field, all the neighboring houses, and further — seven miles at least — to the millstacks and stone church of Lawrence. The work is all inside now. My father's desk is covered with paper, and we bend over the columns of wages, sales, net worth, and assets — the mute, unalterable facts of the finished year. If only the coming one were as solid and clear. He is getting too old for the work. Some days, lifting his head from the ciphers, even he admits it: "I'm not going to do this next year. I'll just prune the fruit trees and seed the fields with hay." Other days he'll say he wants to plant new peach trees on the northeast slope of the orchard come spring.

We watch the clear drop poised at the end of the branch and wait for it to fall into the thawing stream. If we begin again, we'll have no choice but to see it through to the end. The seedlings warming in the greenhouse, in damp peaty growing mix describe a certain and exacting path. We only work alongside, putting one foot in front of the other, and by high summer we can't see beyond the near woods. We can't see the far fields.

Sometimes I think we have too much time in winter. Too much time to mull over numbers. Time to consider our place. Time to exaggerate our fears the way reasonable people do during a sleepless night — there's a presence behind them, a presence in the shadows, and no way to return to the journey of their dreams.

Yes, he can think about what to do all winter, but all he knows how to do is to continue. Already the seed order trickles in, and I find stray packets underneath the papers on the desk — the small crops — Nantes Carrots, say, or Detroit Reds. And here are the Lady Bell Peppers. I lift the packet up and my father says, "That seed cost me forty-five dollars." One quarter ounce. Germination rate: ninety-four percent. It will produce fifteen hundred plants. The nursery will set them in cell packs, which I'll be able to carry in my two hands. We'll transplant them into pots which will take up half the greenhouse, and when the ground warms up enough to plant them, they'll range across a quarter of the back field. People from town will buy them, people will come out from Lawrence, and some from even further. Those plants will yield green peppers and red, sweet peppers that will have to be picked every other day from July to the frost.

✦ ✦ ✦

My first published poem was written so long ago now I've lost track of it, though I remember it was a lyric about the summer fields. My father and Pete were mentioned in it, and when I showed it to my father, after a short silence, he smiled and said — half to himself — "Who'd ever have thought poor Pete would end up in a poem?" Since that time he's occasionally asked, "How many poems did you write today?" or "How much do they pay you for these?" And I mumble across the gulf of lives lived differently: "Oh, I really didn't finish anything today . . ." or "Well, you know, it's not like plowing a field . . ."

I can see him laboring to fit my answers in with his own idea of work, of a steel blade cutting through the thick April rye, and his wake of turned-up earth. One works by going back and forth as the sun arcs across the spring sky, and there's sheer physical exhaustion at the end of the day. Against which all I can muster is: "You get a different kind of tired."

My mother keeps most of her thoughts to herself, though once she said, "It's always about the farm, isn't it?" I bring her most of the work I've published, and she looks at my name on the back of a journal and shuffles through the pages — she'll read them later, never in front of me — then sets it on the coffee table along with *Woman's Day*, various catalogs, and the Boston paper. Or she'll hand it to my father, who'll thumb through until he comes to my work. This last time he looked at the magazine and said: "How about that. You see — there's more to life than planting tomatoes."

It's strange for me to hear that, with its hint, I think, of regret about his own path. He is forever telling me farming is a hard way to make a living, forever warning me away. But I also know he is ingrained in this world, and for him there is no other. Every time I suggest we fold our hand here, he won't hear it.

So much of what he remembers is full of savor, as much as the winter apples in their cellar or the wild grapes in summer. Seventy-five years collapse when he says, "I remember helping Pop plant the potatoes — I couldn't keep up with him — I wasn't more than ten. He'd dig the holes and I would run along behind him and drop the seed potatoes in — right there, where we planted the Hubbards last year." And just yesterday he brought up the hurricane again, this time a story I have never heard, about the orchard he had planted not many years before the storm, and how the wind half-uprooted his trees so that they listed eastward. "I collected the downed wires — they were everywhere — and used them to stake the trees back upright . . ."

A story just told, and, soon, that one too will go untold. What, then, will be made of these times? Will they be remembered? There are years of sleep between the sparked stories, and every time I try to trace it — just when I think what's recollected shines — it shifts, and takes a shape I have never seen.

So much to tell, and even with all the quiet of winters here, there doesn't seem to be enough time. The connections between things takes so long to become apparent. I always seem to want to say more than I'm able to set down. I put down the words, then take them back. Go down a different path. Work, senses, anger, the rust, the relics, the seeds. To give everything its true weight, and not to weigh the anger more than its measure.

Cold and still this morning, and a fine, dry snow has started to fall, deepening the winter cover on the field I see when I look up from my work, the same field where only a few months ago Sallie and I untied a thousand trellised tomatoes, and the spent plants collapsed one after the other at our feet. Now I see white falling into white, and beyond, the sagging side of a disused barn, its paint gone gray. Few sounds come in from outside other than the small worryings of the nuthatches and chickadees, and — muffled by the storm glass — the long hush of traffic. Indoors, too, is cauled in quiet. Key clicks no louder than the songless birds, and soft lead scratching out words.

I know how it will be when the wind comes up at dusk. The snow drifts just as if it were fine sand, and off the crest of those drifts, a handful of snow swirls up and sweeps across the open fields. It keeps an upright shape for a moment, then scatters and is tossed up into the starhung night.

6

LEAVING

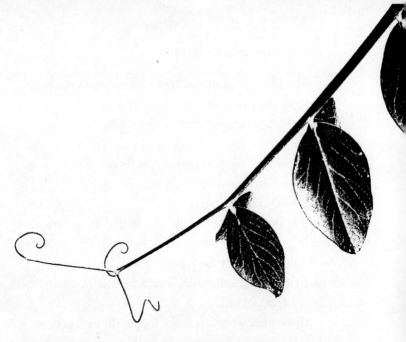

A DRY WEIGHT. A small measure. But in the right hands, even a winter seed speaks for itself. In the still of every January, my father gathers up the seeds from a Hubbard cut up months ago. He takes the corners of the newspaper they are lying on and makes a funnel to slip them into a mason jar. There's always talk that seems to go with it: "That first Hubbard, the flesh was the width of my hand. I saw it in the Boston market — fifty years ago. I said I'd buy the whole squash — it was forty, forty-five pounds, but that I wanted the seed, too." Another time I remember him saying, "One year I sent some seed to Agway — they gave it a field trial, they said, but it didn't yield enough for them. Imagine that. . ." His face brightens as he speaks, just as when he's talking with his sister or brothers. He tightens the lid and labels the jar with masking tape. The best squash won't have a lot of seed, and they usually fill the jar halfway.

One year he spent much of November in the hospital — in Boston — and my mother couldn't negotiate the traffic, so almost every day I'd take her there for a visit.

"How are things at home?" he'd ask.

"Fine," my mother would always say.

"How's Sam doing?"

"He was in for lunch yesterday. How are you feeling?"

"Oh, lazy. They keep poking me. They wake me all night to check something or to take some blood . . . Don't ever get old."

My mother would sit at the foot of the bed, her ankles crossed, her purse clutched in her lap. They'd talk about the weather. My sister. The news. I'd look to see if the numbers on his chart had changed. He'd tell me what bills he was expecting, which ones to pay, and which ones to wait on. I'd ask about his creatinine level and his iron level as if we'd talked about such things, too, for our entire lives.

The one time I went to see him on my own, he was half in and half out of sleep, and his voice was groggy when he asked, "How's Mom holding up?"

"She's OK," I said.

"Make sure you check the oil in the car for her, and the pressure on that front tire."

I remember voices in the hallway. Someone wheeled a cart by, and the glass vials chinked against one another.

"Did Sam sell the Hubbard yet?"

"It's still in the shed, but he put a tarp over it. It'll be OK for awhile, unless it gets really cold."

"But it's going to get cold. He's got to get rid of it before Thanksgiving. There won't be any market after that."

We heard a nurse in the next room saying, *You have to keep the patch on, Mr. Browning.*

My father said, "I still need some seed for next year."

"Do you want me to put some squash aside for you?"

"A few. You can put them in my cellar and I'll break them up when I get home." I couldn't begin to imagine him lifting the Hubbards or taking the cleaver to them, but I said nothing. I just nodded as he told me to make sure they were heavy for their size — the paler ones. No bruises.

He closed his eyes for awhile and then said, "You should be going before the traffic gets too heavy." The color in the eastern sky was already deepening. Thousands of lit windows defined the skyline. I gazed out on the quiet river and Beacon Hill as I put on my coat. I heard him say, "I remember when the State House was the biggest thing on the horizon." What I saw was a small dome distinguished only by the mild luster of its gold leaf, and nearly drowned among the office buildings. A memory in the same place, the world surrounding it changed. As I turned to leave he said, "If anything happens just pull in the tent around you."

There was frost on the tarp, but the squash beneath it had stayed warm enough. I'd say there were at least four ton nested together in one big pile. I walked around the circumference and saw many that would be fine for seed, but they were all mixed in with ones of lesser quality, and I had to lift and shift parts of the pile. The squash were awkward and heavy and not easy for me to handle. Some I could barely manage. And there were beautiful large ones that, when I picked them up, felt lighter than they should. Heavy for its size, he had said . . .

My labored breath plumed into the cold air. The road was quiet, the rye paled with rime. Sometimes I hear what I want. Behind me, a scattering of oak leaves scraped across the pavement, and for a moment they were the footfalls of someone coming towards me.

*   *   *

This week's talk is about cemetery plots. My father has bought the last four in the cemetery, half way up the hill, behind the white birch. From there you can look straight across the late land to the sheds, the stand, the farmhouse. "At least I think I bought them," he tells me. "Carroll, when he arranged for it, had his bottle with him. But I wrote him out a check. He said he'd mail me the deed."

I make a joke about how I want my ashes scattered into the ocean. But he can imagine nothing other than lying in the lee of his farm. My mother will lie there too, even if it's a Protestant cemetery. And Sam. Though after my father is gone, it isn't likely to look out on farmland for long.

Sometimes my father talks of the future as if there were still a clear path. He says to me: "Someone could make a good living here if they're willing to work hard." Maybe it's really his way of speaking about our own lost chances. Though I don't think it's that we haven't worked hard enough. This failure is smaller than that. Smaller than the economy or the weather. Too much silence. Questions that echoed, and went unanswered. And anger thrown into the day's work the way Sam boots a shovel into clay soil. Moments of anger, misunderstandings, and silence accreting over the years until they've become as large as the pines that now shade the eastern edge of the orchard. Their shadows have assumed and deepened the slighter shadows of the apple trees, and hold the frost well into the fall mornings.

A failure that's come on so gradually we took it as usual, and then inevitable. Just like the old horse-drawn coach we left out in the weather. I have no trouble picturing it, the way it listed to its right side. All the times I tried to count the wooden spokes, or gazed at the way my face distorted in the beveled edge of the oblong windows. It stood by the stand for years, a conversation piece for the customers, something children would rush up to just to sway on its handles, and jump on its velvet cushions. A man would come by off and on down the years wanting to buy it and refurbish it. "Not for sale," my father would tell him, and no more than that.

Of course it moldered away, though I seem to remember vague talk about restoring it. My sister had a friend . . . But really by the time such talk surfaced, the wood was already badly weathered, and the metalwork was caked with rust. At last only the glass was fully in-tact. It would have taken a special eye at that point to save it, and more work than anyone could imagine. It crumbled through one winter, and collapsed in a gray pile in the snow. Gone its grace, though we all remem-ber it, and the way we loved to climb in and out of it.

  🐦   🐦   🐦

I wish it was August and the corn was running together, and there wasn't enough help, and Sam and I had ar-gued and argued. But it's January. The work and argu-ments have settled down, and what I say comes out of a long-thought-out silence. I tell my father: "I just can't work with Sam anymore."

He must have known this decision was coming — his voice is small, too, as he says, "He's my son." Then, "I guess it wasn't meant to be." Not much more talk than that — my mother greets my decision with silence, and believes, I think, I'll still relent. Sam — Sam just shrugs his shoulders and walks off.

All the voices: *I figured you'd be opening soon — I saw the corn tasseling out . . . Tomatoes — finally . . . The peaches taste sweeter this year . . .* They are all alive in my mind right next to the old questions. *What's to come? Has my being back here changed anything? Maybe it's made things harder for everyone.* Alive in the long evenings when I wonder how it would be if Sam never dreamed tigers

were stalking him. I try to imagine how he would fare
in the world, and what kind of job he'd hold down.

Finally, when it grows late, and I just can't worry anymore, I come back to my red-eyed justifications: *The
land is tired, a long stretch of fallow years would be the best
thing* . . . Balm for a hundred tiny cuts, yes, but it can't
take care of my anger. I remember pounding on the
truck horn to wake him, and I clench my teeth just as
then, and mutter to myself as I always have: "I *won't* be
my brother's keeper."

It's Orion's evening season, and the air is so clear I can
see Betelgeuse for the red giant it is. Even with the bitter cold, I can't help but take in the sky for awhile before
I step into my parents' quiet low-lit house. If I have dinner with them now, we finish more quickly than before.
With no more easy talk about the farm, I think of how
frail they seem, I hear the sound of silverware scraping
the china. The refrigerator kicks on. My father hunts
up a long story about hauling potatoes out of Maine, or
of the parade in Lawrence on Armistice Day 1918. My
mother asks if I've heard from my sister.

"No, no," I say, "not since last week."

We fall into silence again before I bring up the one
thing so much on my mind:

"Have you thought anymore about next season?
Why don't you just let the fields lie? You could rent out
the orchard easily enough if you wanted to. Or you
could just keep the trees pruned."

"What will Sam do?" my mother asks.

"Sam can figure things out for himself." They say nothing, and I continue: "You could plant enough for the family — a block of corn, a dozen tomato seedlings. Beans. Carrots. Those Knight peas you like so much."

It's hard, even for me, to imagine such a pared-down future. The snowed-in fields are immense, and any small attempt would seem no bigger than candlelight against a starless night. But I prattle on, anyhow, about how he wouldn't have to plant beets again, until my father's temper grows short and he says, "That's enough — I haven't made any decision yet."

The cold months wear on, and I keep at the subject — a winter finch at her seed. I've brought it up again today, and after my father's temper flares and subsides, I promise myself that I'll hold my tongue from now on. "Drive me up to the apple cellar — please," he asks. "Your mother wants some Baldwins." We're quiet in the truck, and when I come to a slow stop by the cellar door, he takes a long time getting out. He is eighty-three. By now both knees are bad, and he is stone blind in one eye. No sound other than his walking stick striking the ground. Then he says, "I worry where people will get their corn."

☙ ☙ ☙

Late snow. Late spring. But finally I hear a call longer than the two notes of winter, and the earth gives beneath my feet. Mist rises off the last stretches of snow — the day is shifting mist — and pours down the gradual slope of the orchard to catch in the branches of the pear, it curls into the harboring pines and thins across souring ice on the pond. Mist obscures the barn and yard and carriage house, then shifts towards the rye, and our buildings suddenly appear clearer than I remember.

To our north the deepest snowpack in years has begun to melt. Already the streams are breaching their familiar channels, and once the rains begin water will erode new beds across the fields, taking soil and subsoil and stones with it. Water to deepen the stains on the walls and slate graves, and to illumine the clear gray bark of the beech. Water to release the scent, bitter and spiced, of decaying oak leaves, bitter mixed with a sweet trace from long dormant corms sending up shoots beside the well. Water to drown out all the other sounds of the thaw — of ice breaking up, of the melt running off six eaves, and of far water falling down a granite outcrop. Voices, too, it drowns out, even the raised ones, and the jangling of the harrow — every chink and scrape the tools make.

I want the sound of water right up next to my ears. Once it stops this time, I'm not sure of the sounds I'll hear, not of a disk striking new stone, not of the shovel pitching into earth, not voices carrying across the spring plantings — "OK." "That's good." "There."

♪　♪　♪

To reach here I've made my way among countless white birches. The woods are full of their light touch, as they are every May. Their pale new leaves, lit by the sun, glint when they shiver, and — above me — sound mild as subsided water coursing over mossy stones. They're not old. The trunks are all nearly the same — tall, slender, unbranched — and the white bark lights the shadows. In a breeze they sway in unison, as if tethered to the same root, and moved by the same mover.

One oak looms from out of them. So late in spring, and everything about it still suggests winter — a few of last year's coppery leaves cling to its branches, and the ones on the ground beneath it are tough and so slow to decay that I step on years of them. The dry rustle I make as I walk sounds out of time — Canada mayflowers and starflowers are already pushing up through the duff.

As yet, there are no new leaves, and all the limbs are apparent. The lowest ones branch out nearly horizontal to the massive trunk, and every one — there are many — crags as it extends. A few of the limbs are long dead, and on the living, the pale gray bark is furrowed, hung with moss and fungus, and crusted with lichen. The crown itself spreads wide and is higher than any other tree in these woods.

Already hundreds of years old, it may last uncounted more. I know there were others, a line of them that once marked a roadway or skirted the boundaries of a field back when this was a more open land. Maybe spared by sentiment or reverence, this one outlived them all. It's hard to believe that some hadn't thought to fell it at one time or another, since oak had been used for everything from ships to hafts even if it needed long, careful curing to keep it from warping. By now, this one is decayed and crooked enough to have escaped such uses. It keeps its own place, far and rarely seen, nearly forgotten.

Its lower branches are the only horizontal lines on this hillside, and so through the birches I can discern it from far off. I head straight there — it's what I've come here to see. A willful presence that takes all my attention, a tough-minded ancestor checking my enthusiasm. And all that shimmers of spring — the new leaves and their sound and the sweet air — drops away.

In another month the birch leaves will have darkened, and the oak will be in full leaf, nearly blended in with the young woods around it. It will seem more of a kind. My somber, ponderous thoughts will go too, becoming far and faint as the sailors' curses who blamed the oak itself, instead of the hasty seasoning, when their ships fell apart on the seas.

Epilogue

THIS YEAR Sallie has a cataract in her right eye. She has to finish trellising the tomatoes, she says, before she sees the doctor on Thursday. The twine, all measured and cut, the color of straw in the sun, hangs over one of the trellis wires. She takes a handful and drapes them over her shoulder. As she moves down the row of transplants she pulls a length of twine from her shoulder, stoops, and ties it around the base of the tomato plant. She weaves the young plant around it and ties the twine to the wire above. She trellises two and then takes a step down the row. When I look up from my desk every now and again, I see her incremental progression.

The winter was a fairly steady time with the farm quiet, buried, still, like every other place, but now that it has come to life, I sometimes feel hemmed in by the goings-on. It's hard for me not to feel as if I should be helping out. I stay inside most of the day, and work in my study. Late in the afternoon, when I know Sam is deep in his house, and the help gone home, I walk down the mail road and into the woods, looking for small things — the overwintered partridgeberries or the lady's-slippers beneath the pines.

As I loop back home I sometimes stop in to see my parents. These past few weeks my father has been talking about his asparagus. There are stray beds of it all over the farm — asparagus grows out of my mother's rosebed, on a knoll in the apple orchard, in my Uncle Cal's abandoned garden in back of the farmhouse. There are a few stray stalks amid the grapevines. Old plantings, out of which he cuts a handful of spears every few days. I know he is just glad to be moving around after the shut-in months.

Changes soon, I know. Even if I have nothing to do with the daily workings of the farm, I know I'll have much to do with those changes. When my sister comes down for a visit, we always seem to find ourselves talking about the future of this place. How much you'd have to do to pay the taxes. Who might want to rent the orchard. But such talk has no real weight. It doesn't even begin to touch on the days ahead. Winters are harder on my parents every year. Where Sam is in the future, I don't know.

I can still feel that my returning here has only delayed what was inevitable, and that we've all returned to our old places, which had been set for years: me in my own life; Sam, no matter how stricken, running the farm. Angry, frustrating hours when I feel I've had no choice but to give in. Though there are times, too, when I'm relieved not to be tied to the daily responsibilities of the farm. How could I have handled things here anyway? There's so much I would have had to learn. I would have had to set aside most of the other dreams I have. Dreams which grow more vivid as my plans pare off from the farm. Ideas for books I want to write. More and more time at my desk.

Still, I can't imagine this place as anything other than a farm. Now there is waning light in the trees. The orchard has just been mowed, and everywhere is the scent of cut grass. Out of the long dusk the call of a thrush defines the edge of the cleared land.

NOTES

Some of the names of family members and other figures in this story have been changed.

I am indebted to many books for understanding and inspiration. Among them are Betty Flanders Thomson's *The Changing Face of New England* (New York: Macmillan, 1958), William Cronon's *Changes in the Land: Indians, Colonists, and the Ecology of New England* (New York: Hill and Wang, 1983), Paul Hudon's *The Valley and Its Peoples* (Windsor Publications, 1982), *Indian New England Before the Mayflower* (Hanover: University Press of New England, 1980) and *A Long Deep Furrow: Three Centuries of Farming in New England* (Hanover: University Press of New England, 1982) both by Howard S. Russell, and *A Natural History of Trees* (Boston: Houghton Mifflin, 1991) by Donald Culross Peattie.

DATE DUE

FEB 1 8 2005	
APR 30 2013	

GAYLORD   PRINTED IN U.S.A.